AFTERSHOCK

AFTERSHOCK

The Halifax Explosion and the Persecution of Pilot Francis Mackey

JANET MAYBEE

NIMBUS
PUBLISHING
NIMBUS.CA

Nimbus Publishing Limited
3731 Mackintosh St, Halifax, NS B3K 5A5
(902) 455-4286 NIMBUS.CA

Printed and bound in Canada
NB1179

Cover Photo: Digitally restored by Joel Zemel (Pilot Francis Mackey). From the Collection of the Maritime Museum of the Atlantic (*Mont Blanc* in Halifax, 1900).

Design: JVDW Designs
All family photos provided courtesy of the Mackey and Dobson grandchildren. All uncredited colour photos provided by Janet Maybee.

Library and Archives Canada Cataloguing in Publication

Maybee, Janet, author
Aftershock : the Halifax explosion and the persecution of
pilot Francis Mackey / Janet Maybee.
Includes bibliographical references and index.
Issued also in electronic format.
ISBN 978-1-77108-344-7 (paperback).—ISBN 978-1-77108-345-4 (html)
1. Halifax Explosion, Halifax, N.S., 1917. 2. Explosions—Nova Scotia—
Halifax—History—20th century. 3. Mackey, Francis, 1872-1961. 4. Pilots
and pilotage—Nova Scotia—Halifax—History—20th century. 5. Halifax
(N.S.)—History—20th century. I. Title.

FC2346.4.A38 2015   971.6'22503   C2015-904333-6
C2015-904334-4

Nimbus Publishing acknowledges the financial support for its publishing activities from the Government of Canada through the Canada Book Fund (CBF) and the Canada Council for the Arts, and from the Province of Nova Scotia. We are pleased to work in partnership with the Province of Nova Scotia to develop and promote our creative industries for the benefit of all Nova Scotians.

Gratefully dedicated to Janet Kitz, whose research preserved the stories of Halifax Explosion survivors, whose writing sparked interest in this vital information locally and around the world, and whose wisdom continues to inspire new explorers.

CONTENTS

Psalm 23, Mariner's Version

The Lord is my Pilot
I shall not drift.
He leadeth me across the dark waters
and steereth me in the deep channels.
He keepeth my Log
And guideth me by the star of holiness
for His Name's sake.
Yea, though I sail amid
the thunders and tempests of life,
I shall dread no danger,
for Thou art with me;
Thy love and Thy care, they shelter me.
Thou preparest a harbour before me
in the homeland of eternity;
Thou anointest the waves with oil,
And my ship rideth calmly,
· Surely sunlight and starlight
shall favour me all the days of my voyaging,
and I will rest in the port of my Lord forever.

—The Mast, *September 1948*

FOREWORD

*"It has been said of the native people, upon the arrival of
Champlain, that they approached his vessel in their canoes
leading the way in to Saint John and warning of the dangers
of the Reversing Falls at the mouth of the river. In effect, the
native people of the area were indeed the first pilots here."*

—*She's All Yours Mr. Pilot: The Marine Pilots of Saint John*,
Captain Donald Duffy and Neil McKelvey, o.c., q.c.

Marine pilotage is one of the oldest professions in the world, with references to pilots found in some of the earliest recorded history. In Europe, a pilot was originally known as a "lodesman," derived from "lodestone," a naturally occurring magnet that was used as an early compass. The word "pilot" evolved from Dutch terminology describing a plumb lead used for measuring the depth of water. But the first marine pilots in Atlantic Canada were undoubtedly the Mi'kmaq.

Over their many thousands of years in this region, the Mi'kmaq navigated their sea canoes through the coastal waters of Atlantic Canada. They were known to travel in the Bay of Fundy and the Northumberland Strait, to cross the Cabot Strait between Nova Scotia and Newfoundland, and to spend summers in the sheltered fishing grounds of Bedford Basin and Halifax Harbour. The first

European observers of their skill believed the Mi'kmaq were guided by instinct, but it surely had more to do with the people's local knowledge of currents, tides, and navigational hazards. This local knowledge remains at the core of marine pilotage to this day.

Early explorers often used the skills of the Mi'kmaq to pilot their ships into these uncharted waters. However, when Edward Cornwallis arrived to establish

A pilot schooner in Purcell's Cove, 1890. ATLANTIC PILOTAGE AUTHORITY

Halifax in 1749, he was not able to take advantage of the local knowledge of the Mi'kmaw people, likely because of their allegiance to the French forces at that time. His ship, the *Sphinx*, stayed offshore because there was no pilot to help guide it into the harbour. On June 21, a full week later, a passing ship en route from Boston to Louisbourg was hailed, and it was found there were two pilots on board. One of these mariners piloted the *Sphinx* into port. Within a year, a pilotage service was established in Halifax. It remained unregulated, however, until 1826, when the legislative assembly of the colony passed an act regulating pilotage and requiring pilots to successfully pass a licensing examination.

During the First World War the volume of vessel traffic in Halifax Harbour increased tremendously, while the number of pilots available remained stable. Pilots saw their workloads double or, in some cases, triple during the war. One pilot, who kept a meticulous diary of his activity, had more pilotage assignments in 1917 alone than he had in the four-year period from 1911 through 1914 inclusive.

Two pilot schooners, owned jointly by active and retired pilots and the estates of deceased pilots, were used in Halifax as pilot boats in 1917. The pilots' earnings for each month would be divided in equal shares after providing one and a half shares to the operation of the pilot boats. Manned by apprentice pilots, an engineer, a cook, and seamen, these schooners were designed to accommodate approximately fifteen persons at a time. The ships would take turns on duty, week about, with one schooner staying near the pilot boarding station and the other being berthed in the harbour. Small tenders manned by the crew of the pilot schooner transferred pilots to and from ships.

The pilots worked on a roster system and, after taking a ship out of the harbour, would stay on the pilot schooner until their turn came to pilot a ship back in. During peacetime, with both less vessel activity and urgency, the pilots would often enjoy some off-duty time at home with their families in between assignments. During the First World War, however, with the exception of occasional lulls in activity, all pilots were expected to be on duty.

With marine radio communication being in its infancy in 1917, pilots had to rely on audible and visual cues such as steam whistles, signals, and flags to determine what course an oncoming vessel was intending to steer. The propulsion systems on ships at that time would be considered very rudimentary today: most had steam engines or steam turbines driving a single propeller. And radar and electronic navigation systems were, of course, many years away. As for navigational aids, pilots had to rely on lighthouses, leading lights, and local landmarks to allow them to safely maneuver a vessel.

Pilots in 1917 would have also had navigation charts, the origins of which may be surprising. Captain James Cook was a world-renowned explorer in the Pacific during the eighteenth century; it is not as well known, however, that he developed his skill as a cartographer in Atlantic Canada, and created detailed and precise nautical charts that were used, in some cases, for over two hundred years. Pilots down through the years have used his charts with confidence and owe him a debt of gratitude.

Those employed by the Atlantic Pilotage Authority today have many advantages over the pilots of 1917: they certainly have much more advanced navigation equipment and propulsion systems on ships, they no longer live on the pilot boat while on duty, and modern, fast pilot boats take them to and from ships. In Halifax, a weather buoy provides real-time information on wind speed and direction, significant and maximum wave height, and peak-wave period. Data obtained from this buoy is combined with other meteorological information to provide a precise forecast, including wind and wave outlooks several days in advance (see smartatlantic.ca).

But although they have these advantages, today's pilots face many of the same challenges as their predecessors did in 1917. Early twentieth-century pilots must have had an encyclopedic local knowledge of their harbour, must have possessed expert ship-handling skills, and must have been prepared to accept the challenges of hostile weather and inhospitable working hours. Modern shipping occurs in Halifax Harbour at any hour of the day and night, and in virtually all weather conditions. The contemporary pilot must handle ships that are much larger and more sophisticated than those of his predecessors, and also must deal with increasing cultural and language barriers, as shipping has become a much more globalized industry.

The professional pilots employed by the Atlantic Pilotage Authority have thorough knowledge of the local pilotage area, including port infrastructure and subsurface characteristics. They must have knowledge of the handling characteristics of each type of vessel calling on their port so that they will be able to accurately judge the effect of wind, current, wave, and tidal influences on the ship

Two Halifax pilot boats currently in service, at the wharf and always at the ready.
©SANDY McCLEARN

<small>Atlantic Pilotage Authority</small>

they are piloting. And they must maintain good physical condition, so they can safely transfer between a ship and a pilot boat in adverse sea states and weather conditions.

Pilotage has evolved over the centuries, and will continue to evolve with expanding technology and knowledge. It remains today a noble and necessary profession; indeed, one that carries with it a great deal of responsibility and public trust.

—Peter MacArthur, Chief Financial Officer
of the Atlantic Pilotage Authority
January 2015

PREFACE

For a hundred years Pilot Francis Mackey, a skilled and experienced harbour pilot, has unfairly borne blame for the disastrous Halifax Explosion of December 6, 1917. Mackey chanced to be the pilot assigned to bring a munitions ship, *Mont Blanc*, into Bedford Basin that morning; a departing relief vessel, *Imo*, travelling on the wrong side of the harbour, collided with *Mont Blanc* and the resulting fire led to a blast that killed at least two thousand innocent citizens, injured twelve thousand, left perhaps twice that number homeless, and caused $35 million in damage to the city and harbour facilities.

After a brutal Wreck Commissioner's Inquiry, Francis Mackey was accused of manslaughter and criminal negligence, jailed, and vilified in the headlines of local newspapers. Despite his eventual release by a judge who found absolutely no evidence to support these charges, it seemed there were federal authorities determined to keep the pilot in the useful role of scapegoat. The federal minister of Marine, C. C. Ballantyne, adamantly refused to return Mackey's pilot's license and allow him to work as a pilot. And over the next several months attempts were made by three Halifax officials, the Crown Prosecutor, the Attorney General and the Chief of Police, to drag Mackey back before a jury. The cost of legal counsel while supporting his large and growing family was a huge burden for an unemployed pilot. His ongoing punishment, which Mackey himself described as persecution, was severe and undeserved.

This book is not a Halifax Explosion report. There are many excellent records, some written by people who were present that day: Thomas Raddall, Archibald

MacMechan, Samuel Prince, and others were witnesses. Photographers captured horrific images of the devastation, perhaps none more powerful than the sketches of Arthur Lismer, a founding member of the Group of Seven and principal of the Victoria School of Art and Design, which later became NSCAD. With the exception of Hugh MacLennan's novel *Barometer Rising* (1941), Michael Bird's *The Town That Died* (1967), Mary Ann Monnon's *Miracles and Mysteries* (1977), and Graham Metson's *The Halifax Explosion* (1978), there followed a decade of silence until diligent researcher Janet Kitz began her explorations in the 1980s. Gathering survivors together, many who had never described their experiences to anyone, Kitz freed them to speak in the safe company of others. She collected their stories and undertook the painful task of studying the mortuary bags, the pitiful remnants of lives erased. Her books, *Shattered City* (1989) and *Survivors* (1992), heralded a surge of interest in all aspects of explosion lore.

In the late twentieth century, Halifax began to honour this tragic part of its history with monuments and memorials: a bell tower was created on Fort Needham

The Hour of Horror in Devastated Richmond

Arthur Lismer's sketch, titled *The Hour of Horror in Devastated Richmond*, published in Stanley K. Smith: *The Drama of a City; the Story of Stricken Halifax*, 1918. TORONTO PUBLIC LIBRARY

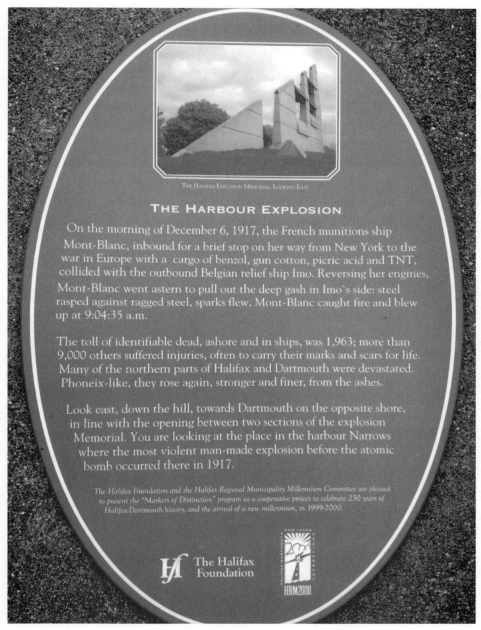

THE HALIFAX EXPLOSION MEMORIAL, LOOKING EAST

THE HARBOUR EXPLOSION

On the morning of December 6, 1917, the French munitions ship Mont-Blanc, inbound for a brief stop on her way from New York to the war in Europe with a cargo of benzol, gun cotton, picric acid and TNT, collided with the outbound Belgian relief ship Imo. Reversing her engines, Mont-Blanc went astern to pull out the deep gash in Imo's side: steel rasped against ragged steel, sparks flew, Mont-Blanc caught fire and blew up at 9:04:35 a.m.

The toll of identifiable dead, ashore and in ships, was 1,963; more than 9,000 others suffered injuries, often to carry their marks and scars for life. Many of the northern parts of Halifax and Dartmouth were devastated. Phoenix-like, they rose again, stronger and finer, from the ashes.

Look east, down the hill, towards Dartmouth on the opposite shore, in line with the opening between two sections of the explosion Memorial. You are looking at the place in the harbour Narrows where the most violent man-made explosion before the atomic bomb occurred there in 1917.

The Halifax Foundation and the Halifax Regional Municipality Millennium Committee are pleased to present the "Markers of Distinction" program as a cooperative project to celebrate 250 years of Halifax-Dartmouth history, and the arrival of a new millennium, in 1999-2000.

The Halifax Foundation

HRM2000

This plaque sits in front of the Memorial Bell Tower at Fort Needham, Unfortunately the names of the ships are reversed, casting blame on *Mont Blanc* and Pilot Mackey.

in 1985, then in 1989 the thousand-pound *Mont Blanc* anchor shaft was mounted near where it landed, more than three kilometres west of the explosion site, while an equally heavy gun sits in Dartmouth, blown five kilometres east. On December 6, 1992, firefighters dedicated a monument at Station 4 in the city's historic north end to honour their heroic colleagues who died responding to the fire alarm with their new engine, the Patricia, seventy-five years earlier.

On that same anniversary in 1992, the Gorsebrook Institute organized an important conference at Saint Mary's University and preserved more than thirty of the wide-ranging papers presented there in the volume *Ground Zero*, unfortunately now out of print and rare. That same year Robert MacNeil published his powerful novel, *Burden of Desire*. Other books followed: historical accounts like Blair Beed's *1917 Halifax Explosion and American Response* and family records such as James and Rowena Mahar's *Too Many to Mourn* (1998), and works of fiction with the explosion as background. The book which broke new ground based on extensive research in Ottawa, where most naval and pilotage records were stored, was John Griffith Armstrong's *The Halifax Explosion and the Royal Canadian Navy* (2002). By the time of the explosion's ninetieth anniversary in 2007, dedicated Halifax researchers Alan Ruffman and Wendy Findley were able to compile a bibliography of more than two hundred resources.

Many websites have been developed and many more books published since then. The CBC produced two fine documentaries and aired one error-filled mini-series in 2003 as well as launching a useful Halifax Explosion website—accurate because the creators had wisely engaged a group of local historians to approve the content. In recognition of the explosion's one-hundredth anniversary (2017), there will undoubtedly be another wave of interest and writings and filmmaking. But there is an important part of the tale that has not yet been told: Francis Mackey, wrongfully arrested, imprisoned, deprived of his livelihood and reputation, was deliberately kept in a kind of purgatory for the four years following the disaster. The stress and shaming he endured unjustly punished his whole family. Historians seem to have assumed, mistakenly, that he went back to his work on the harbour and faded into obscurity. But the real story connects Mackey's personal struggles to the political landscape of the day in a manner that sounds sadly familiar even now.

I will not retrace what others have already presented or repeat the graphic details of destruction, death, or heroism from that terrible time. Instead, I want

Mona Mackey Holmes holds a photo of her parents, Lillian and Francis Mackey, taken in 1900.

to share information never before revealed by members of Mackey's family nor allowed out of federal government vaults, documents that contain evidence of serious federal efforts to cover up Ottawa's responsibility for what happened to Halifax on December 6, 1917. Finally, I must fulfill a promise I made to Mackey's last surviving daughter, Mona Mackey Holmes: I will do my best to clear her father's name and diminish the persistent damage to his reputation and to the well-being of his descendants.

INTRIGUED

I am not part of the Mackey clan, but was fortunate to become connected by chance. In 2007 I bought a house on Cabot Street in the north end of Halifax and learned it had survived the explosion. My curiosity was triggered since I had just finished reading Armstrong's account of the navy's role in that catastrophe and I'd heard the stories of my grandfather, a railway fireman in 1917. As a teacher I had introduced the Kitz books to the school library and to my own classes. No professional historian, I had nonetheless gained a lifelong interest in the city's past while writing a Dalhousie thesis on late nineteenth-century Halifax theatre companies and enjoying the good fortune of a year's employment at the provincial archives. In the newspaper room at that time, pre-microfilm,

Cabot Street house after the explosion, and today.

one could handle the actual papers. I was well acquainted with original press accounts from December 1917 and the dramatic headlines that laid suspicion fiercely on Pilot Mackey. Intrigued, I found two women who had grown up in the Cabot Street house. It was built in 1896 by their maternal grandfather, Arthur Simmons, and I discovered a handwritten list he had submitted to the Explosion Relief Commission for damages of $3,663.45, for shattered walls and windows, destroyed furniture—even the potatoes and turnips frozen in the basement.

Ninety years after the disaster, as I sat at a sunny Grand Desert kitchen table with Marguerite Dobson Richards, her sister Carol Dobson Watters unfolded albums of family photos. One portrait of a rather portly but elegant gentleman caught my attention and I was surprised to hear, "Oh, that's Francis Mackey, our step-grandfather. He visited us often and his widow, our grandmother Margaret, came to live with our parents." In fact, after Mackey's death on December 31, 1961, his second wife had moved into the very Cabot Street room that was now my studio. No wonder I had to pay attention!

In their memories of the retired pilot's conversations, Grandpa Mackey was confident he had done everything he could to avoid the collision. He was proud of the support he had received from fellow pilots and the shipping community; he felt vindicated by his peers. Yet every December around the

Francis Mackey 1939: "That's our step-grandfather!"

anniversary of the explosion he would become silent and withdrawn, unlike his more familiar storytelling, poetry-loving self.

Though he never dwelt on the details of that tragic day, there was one theme that did become familiar to Mackey's family: Frank Mackey always believed his good friend and fellow pilot William Hayes could not have been in charge of *Imo* that morning. They had worked together for twenty years or more and knew each other's signals very well indeed. Hayes would never have insisted on bringing his ship into the channel that rightly belonged to *Mont Blanc*, Mackey was convinced. The grandchildren were not even sure Hayes had been on board *Imo* that morning.

In the archives I found several varying newspaper reports on the discovery of Hayes's body: on Brunswick Street, on the Dartmouth shore by the brewery, even "never found." Eventually the diary of a fellow pilot, Mont Power, settled the question with an entry on December 9, 1917: "boarded s/s Imo and found the body of Pilot Wm. Hayes which was still on the bridge but the bridge was blown from its position."

Presently I introduced myself to Janet Kitz, and learned she had interviewed a daughter of Arthur Simmons, Merita Simmons Dobson, who lived in the Cabot Street house most of her life. Rita knew exactly where she had been that fateful morning: in the kitchen having her braids tidied for her walk to Richmond School, where classes did not begin until 9:30 in winter. They would never start that day. A few seconds before 9:05 A.M., glass fragments from the skylight blew into her hair and scarred her mother's face. The Simmons family took refuge with Rita's grandparents on Robie Street, and when spring came they camped in a barn out back until their home was repaired. It was a farmhouse with a wide open field behind, right up to the city's water tank on top of the hill; nothing else

Belgian Relief ship *Imo* grounded on the Dartmouth shore. FROM THE COLLECTION OF THE MARITIME MUSEUM OF THE ATLANTIC, HALIFAX, NOVA SCOTIA.

except a brook and some free-range hens and a cow or two.

A decade later, Rita Simmons married Gerard Dobson, the son of Pilot Mackey's second wife, and eventually raised four children (including Marguerite and Carol, who first introduced me to the pilot) in that same house. And so it was that Francis Mackey had often visited the house that was now mine, sat at dinner in my dining room, told stories, and recited Rudyard Kipling's "If," a favourite from his repertoire of poems committed to memory.

Janet Kitz encouraged me with news of a Mackey daughter still living in Halifax, but warned that she had refused to give interviews when approached in the 1980s. Cautiously I telephoned, and found a welcome. There followed many delightful visits to Mona Mackey Holmes and her husband, Edwin Holmes, and hours of voice recordings. These stories are of course compressed and edited, but essentially are their own memories, amazing, clear, and detailed, which they shared with patience and generosity. Fortunately the storytelling did not end with Mona's departure in September of 2009; I continued to visit Ed and record more conversations for another three years. His wit and memory remained sharp to the end of his life.

Arthur Simmons in front of the Cabot Street house he built, with sons Percy and Reg and a neighbour.

ABOVE AND LEFT The Simmons children were familiar with farm chores; the cow and the hens could wander up to the wooden water tower on Robie Street. **RIGHT** Merita's brother Percy dug up a large chunk of the shattered *Mont Blanc* in their garden.

BELOW Rita Dobson often took her children camping: Frank, named for his grandfather the pilot, Marguerite, Marie, and Carol.

RIGHT Years later, the family portrait in the formal Cabot Street parlour: Gerard Dobson, Rita, Frank, Marguerite, Marie, and Carol.

If

If you can keep your head when all about you
Are losing theirs and blaming it on you,
If you can trust yourself when all men doubt you,
But make allowance for their doubting too;
If you can wait and not be tired by waiting,
Or being lied about, don't deal in lies,
Or being hated, don't give way to hating,
And yet don't look too good, nor talk too wise:

If you can dream—and not make dreams your master;
If you can think—and not make thoughts your aim;
If you can meet with Triumph and Disaster
And treat those two impostors just the same;
If you can bear to hear the truth you've spoken
Twisted by knaves to make a trap for fools,
Or watch the things you gave your life to, broken,
And stoop and build 'em up with worn-out tools:

If you can make one heap of all your winnings
And risk it on one turn of pitch-and-toss,
And lose, and start again at your beginnings
And never breathe a word about your loss;
If you can force your heart and nerve and sinew
To serve your turn long after they are gone,
And so hold on when there is nothing in you
Except the Will which says to them: 'Hold on!'

If you can talk with crowds and keep your virtue,
Or walk with Kings—nor lose the common touch,
If neither foes nor loving friends can hurt you,
If all men count with you, but none too much;
If you can fill the unforgiving minute
With sixty seconds' worth of distance run,
Yours is the Earth and everything that's in it,
And—which is more—you'll be a Man, my son!

—Rudyard Kipling

Francis Mackey
entertains his
family: Ronald,
Marjorie,
Florence, Aunt
Babe, Mona, and
Eileen.

The more I learned about Francis Mackey and his family, the more unfortunate seemed the public portrayal of this veteran harbour pilot as country bumpkin or illiterate fisherman—or worse still, a heartless, lying, self-serving villain. He was a complex, competent, and intelligent man, as his own words and letters reveal. His descendants remember a meticulous person, well dressed at work and even in his retirement, a careful man who polished the brass on his fishing rods and wrapped his cleaned paintbrushes in paper to dry flat. He was a devout Catholic, a kind father who demanded proper behaviour from his six children, a good-humoured, genial host and entertainer. That charming personality changed, however, on December 6 each year.

Mackey's family remains as baffled as the pilot was by the obstinate denials that greeted his appeals to Ottawa for the return of his pilot's license. Many letters and petitions of support make it absolutely clear he was respected, trusted, and valued by the shipping community and his fellow pilots. Why did Mackey have to spend four years and his life's savings in a battle to regain his license and salvage his reputation?

The storytellers: Edwin Holmes and Mona Mackey Holmes, 2007.

I wanted to find answers.

Two trips to Library and Archives Canada turned up evidence not available in Nova Scotia and in part restricted because of eternal solicitor-client privilege, since the minister of justice acted as solicitor for other federal departments. Eventually this forbidden correspondence between the justice and marine departments was released to me, after more than a year of persistent pleading with the information commissioner and the intervention of a staff person with Nova Scotian roots. With this material I wrote "The Persecution of Pilot Mackey" for *Northern Mariner*, the journal of the Canadian Nautical Research Society.[1]

Visits with Mackey descendants in Montreal, Denyse, Laurette, and Frank Mackey, yielded much more family history and carefully saved copies of letters, legal documents, and photographs. The two daughters of Mona and Ed Holmes, Janet Connolly and Carole Holmes-Lauder, contributed stories, photos,

The Montreal Mackey grandchildren: Paul, Laurette, Frank, and Denyse (a traffic calming consultant, a librarian, an editor/author, and a lawyer), whose father, Douglas, was the youngest of the pilot's children.

---

1   For additional information and details regarding source materials, see "The Persecution of Pilot Mackey" in *Northern Mariner* xx No. 2, (April 2010), 149-173.

and yellowed newspaper clippings. Transcripts of the pilot's testimony at the Wreck Commissioner's Inquiry, his impassioned letters seeking justice, and the discovery of an archived 1958 CBC Radio interview made it possible to recover Mackey's version of the story in his own words.

The final section of this book investigates some of the political and legal background of this complicated tale, beyond what has already been unearthed, proposed, upheld, or refuted by others. My focus is chiefly on what was contained in the secret Ottawa files and in the brown envelopes and small black suitcase of family treasures. It is clear from these sources that Pilot Mackey became a useful lightning rod for public fury, allowing federal officials to escape responsibility.

Every year around the sixth of December there is almost certain to appear a note mentioning that Francis Mackey was pilot of the French vessel which collided with the relief ship in Halifax Harbour and blew up, killing thousands and destroying much of the city. Often such stories report that he was charged with manslaughter and imprisoned; they always fail to mention that he was exonerated. That Pilot Mackey survived many desperate years of persecution and struggle is a testament to his strength. But a hundred years under this cloud is enough: it is time to lift the weight of defamation carried far too long by a man and a family who did not deserve such a burden. It is time to tell Mackey's truth.

One of the poems Francis Mackey had committed to memory was Samuel Taylor Coleridge's *The Rime of the Ancient Mariner*. His grandchildren recall these haunting verses were a significant part of his repertoire.

The boat came closer to the ship,
But I nor spake nor stirred;
The boat came close beneath the ship,
And straight a sound was heard.

Under the water it rumbled on,
Still louder and more dread:
It reached the ship, it split the bay;
The ship went down like lead.

Stunned by that loud and dreadful sound,
Which sky and ocean smote,
Like one that hath been seven days drowned
My body lay afloat;
But swift as dreams, myself I found
Within the Pilot's boat.

Upon the whirl, where sank the ship,
The boat spun round and round;
And all was still, save that the hill
Was telling of the sound.

(Part the Seventh, verses 7–10)

⚓

Chapter 1

WHO WAS FRANCIS MACKEY?

F rancis Mackey was born November 1, 1872, second son of Simon and Sarah Mackey of Ketch Harbour, Nova Scotia. By the time he started apprentice training as a pilot in 1893 he had already spent almost half his life at sea. In our earliest conversations, Mackey's daughter Mona pointed out that by 1917 he'd been taking ships out of the harbour and steering them in for twenty years and never had a problem. "Not a scratch!" she insisted. "And before that he was working on the water from the time he was twelve, first as a cabin boy on the St. Lawrence and then fishing on the Grand Banks with his father. So much experience and he was just forty-five years old. He was a good character." Mona was certain that while her father wasn't well educated, he had to be clever to know the marine laws as well as he did. "The children in the villages got to about

Harbour Pilot Francis Mackey as he always dressed, even for work at sea. DIGITALLY RESTORED BY JOEL ZEMEL.

grade six or eight in those days and that's as far as they went. They had to go to work."

Late in his eighties Mackey told a newspaper reporter about some of those very early experiences. Once, while fishing with his father when he was about sixteen, Mackey fell over the rail of the schooner and was likely to drown, but the air inside his oilskin coat kept him afloat. His sou'wester flew off and drifted in another direction, so the crewmen were looking in the wrong place. They had to stop Simon Mackey from jumping overboard to try to rescue his son before they finally dragged the young fisherman aboard. He recalled by then he was tired of trying to swim and was just bobbing up and down like a cork. Hauled up over the side, a hot drink, a dry shirt, and Mackey went right back to work.

With this adventurous background and his natural intelligence, Francis Mackey had no difficulty with his pilot's license examinations, second-class in 1895 and first-class three years later. He acquired a master's certificate for the coastal trade in 1899, and was therefore the best-qualified pilot working for the Halifax Pilotage Commission in the early 1900s. Members of the commission's board of directors were usually patronage appointees and tended to spend little time on management issues, so the pilots were fairly free to make their own rules and agreements. They set up their own pension fund and shared their substantial and well-deserved earnings. It was difficult and dangerous work in all seasons, and all kinds of weather.

The dangers and challenges multiplied with the onset of the First World War and the huge increase in shipping as convoys gathered in Bedford Basin to transport troops and supplies to Europe. There were no more pilots added to the roster, no additional pilot boats, and a high degree of confusion about who was actually in charge of the harbour: The convoy commander? The captain superintendent? The pre-war harbour master? The British navy? The very modest and barely hatched Canadian navy? The chief examining officer? Inevitably the pilots made their own decisions and Mackey had great confidence in his ability to handle any situation.

With so much uncertainty about the chain of command in the harbour, it was understandable that pilots tended to operate independently. In a 1958 CBC Radio interview, Mackey offered his strong opinions on Ottawa's inadequate management of wartime harbour traffic:

When the war started orders came from Ottawa that ships were not allowed to enter in daylight. After a while the Basin commenced to get full of ships and there were some young pilots that didn't like the idea of going up there in the night. They were leery of getting up there and finding a berth. I knew how to find a berth myself. I could bring a ship into the Basin at night and anchor her between two others, no problem, whether there was room or not, and take her away in the morning.

I had occasion to see Captain Martin at the Dockyard. I said, "What do you think about ships parading back and forth outside all day and not allowed in?" I said "To my mind it's most ridiculous." "Certainly," he said, "It's ridiculous...why, it's wicked! Now," he says, "I'm glad you came in, sit down. My hands are tied, Pilot, I can only act on orders from Ottawa. If you make a statement here and you want it to be taken notice of," he says, "all I can do is send it to Ottawa. I'll write a letter."

He wrote the letter and I worded it all. And he called an orderly to post the letter, and as he was going down the steps of the building, Captain Martin walked over to the window and came back and slammed his fist down on the table and says, "Pilot, this is good enough for a telegram. I'll telegraph." Now all this night business coming in was all changed to daylight the next morning at nine o'clock. That will show you what kinds of things were going on. Blunder after blunder!

It is probably not surprising that after the explosion Ottawa officials were quick to take any opportunity to discredit and silence this outspoken pilot. Federal authorities were not happy with the prospect of being blamed for blunders that led to the disaster just a few weeks later.

In August of 1900 Mackey felt secure enough at last to wed Lillian Wrayton, four years his junior, daughter of a respected sea captain and raised in Halifax's affluent south end. Proposing to the beautiful red-haired Lillian was perhaps a

Engagement photo of Lillian Wrayton and Francis Mackey, 1900.

bold move considering Mackey's own, less sheltered, origins. Family legend has it that this strong Mackey tribe descended from Spanish and Italian fishermen who came ashore to dry their catch, married local girls, and populated Nova Scotian seaside villages such as Portuguese Cove and Herring Cove. The name Mackey used to be Macchia, so Mona was told.

Mackey's parents, Simon and Sarah Mackey, were fisherfolk who eventually moved from Ketch Harbour into the city as Simon took command of bigger vessels. Francis Mackey's grown siblings scattered all over the continent, mostly in search of safer occupations than their father's work on the ocean. Luke, the oldest brother, worked in the shipyards, but Francis was the only son to follow his father to sea. As Mona explained, "Quite a few of my father's brothers and sisters went out west. Sam was a cross-country railroad man, Lucy got married in Winnipeg, and Joe drowned in the Red River when he was only twenty-six. James was a customs agent, I think, with a wooden leg. Might have been handy for bringing bottles across the border from the States!" Her beloved husband, Ed, whose vision was almost gone, could not appreciate Mona's smile and the twinkle of amusement in her eyes, but he shared the laughter.

"Then there was Aunt Babe," added Mona, "my father's youngest sister. Her real name was Loretta and she lived in an apartment on 5th Avenue in New York and sometimes in California. She was a script reader and casting agent for the big movie studio Fox, and she even had a summer place on Fire Island, next door to that movie star Yul Brynner! She never married, but we heard a story or two. She had a fur coat with a leather belt, I remember." Aunt Babe ended her glamorous saga living next door to the Montreal branch of the Mackey clan—her nephew Douglas's family—but as teenagers at the time,

Aunt Babe, adventurous woman of mystery.

his children were not as interested in family history as they later became, and so Aunt Babe's life remains a source of myth and legend.

"Aunt Molly was really Mary Ellen," Mona continued, "And she never married either, lived to be one hundred. She had started out to be a nurse at the mental hospital in Dartmouth but a patient escaped and she hurt her knee chasing him, so she took a typing course and opened a school in Truro, Mack's Business College. She taught two kinds of shorthand. She ended up in Vancouver and her mother, Sarah, eventually came to live with her there."

Not a family of aristocrats, but ambitious, hardworking, and intelligent people, those Mackeys. Francis was darkly handsome and clearly successful in his piloting career, which probably helped the Wraytons overcome any misgivings they might have felt about handing the lovely Lillian over to a Ketch Harbour man.

Their marriage was by all accounts a happy and productive one. They lived first on Fenwick Street in Halifax's south end, and then bought a comfortable four-bedroom home at 382 Robie Street across from Camp Hill, where in 1917 a new hospital for returning war veterans had just been built. By December 6 of that year the couple had launched five children and had a sixth on the way.

Their lives seemed blessed with good fortune. But the terrible events of that day destroyed many Halifax families and the Mackeys did not escape damage. Not just windows were broken, but hearts too.

After his retirement Captain Mackey enjoyed weekly visits from his daughter Mona's thoughtful husband, Ed, who tried to arrive on the afternoons when Mrs. Mackey (the pilot's second wife, not Mona's mother) was away grocery shopping. It seemed Mackey could speak more freely in his wife's absence, and Ed suspected she was weary of hearing those explosion memories. Even after years as part of the family, Ed never addressed Frank Mackey as anything other than Captain, and still recalled how nervous he had been when asking permission to marry the pilot's treasured daughter. For one thing, the Mackeys were a strong Catholic family and Ed was Protestant. Ed also recognized how close Mona had been with her father growing up, even though she definitely had a mind of her own. It was heartwarming to hear him tell stories of their courtship: "I'll never forget how Mona came to meet me for the first time, across the Northwest Arm in a borrowed canoe, even though her sister reminded her she already had

Courtship days: Mona and Ed, late 1930s.

a boyfriend named Ed. 'I'll see whoever I please,' she told Marjorie, and came along. When she stepped on shore with her red-gold hair shining I said, 'That's the woman I will marry!' A good decision; lasted seventy years."

Ed valued Captain Mackey as a great storyteller who could describe in vivid detail the hard life of a pilot. He'd explain how a group of them would go out on the pilot schooner and stay a week at a time off Chebucto Head, where they took turns on duty as the ships came and went. Or how they went barehanded even in the worst of winter because wool mittens would freeze to the rope ladders they had to climb up to the deck. Or that sometimes it would be too stormy to get back safely to the pilot boat and twice he got carried away on an outgoing ship, first to New York and then to England. (Mona recalled her delight: "Father brought back presents!")

One of Mackey's favourite tales of triumph concerned a challenging race to free a grounded ship and get away to fetch coal for the troop ship RMS *Olympic.* This episode took place around November 16, 1917, just three weeks before the explosion. Ed was pleased to hear it again when I played Mackey's CBC recording for him, nodding his head with every familiar line.

There was a wicked high wind and ships were going ashore. I took one off of Georges Island and took her down to get a load of bunker coal for the *Olympic* in Louisburg. Ice there too, winter had set in. *Sarah Radcliffe* was the name of the ship. I went to take her down but she had dragged ashore on the north side of Georges Island. Well, they were coming down foolish from the dockyard with tugs. I went aboard and the Captain was a young fellow parading up and down and I says, "Captain, what's the matter?"

"Why," he says, "Pilot, we're ashore."

"Good place to be," I says, "last night." We'd had a wind north-northeast and she bogged down in soft mud and some fine gravel. She rested right there.

I climbed aboard the bow up the rope ladder off the tug and instead of going to Louisbourg right that morning I didn't get away till the next morning. Where she touches the ground of course we had to be surveyed no matter if there's not a scratch on her. "Well," I says,

"Captain don't you worry, I'll tell you what you do: you take this tug and go up to the dockyard and see Commander Holloway, he's the transport officer. Tell him who's aboard of your ship, tell him Mackey is aboard of your ship." We were friendly and he knew what I was about. "Tell him I'll bring the ship off at half past nine tonight." That was when it would be the right tide.

Down came a tug from the dockyard with wires and hawsers of all kinds and they said, "Where would you like to have us tonight? We heard you were coming off at half past nine and we'll give you all the help you require."

I says, "No need of help, all I want from you is to keep away from my stern! I'm going to bring this ship off on her own steam at half past nine tonight."

They went back to the Dockyard and they came back later again. "Here we are again, Pilot. Well you don't want any hawsers? You know we've got good new ones here."

"Not at all," I said, "No hawsers. Keep away from my stern."

"Well we got orders to look after doing it."

I said, "If you want to look at scenery, then all right."

So when the time came, I knew how she was lying with starboard side against the bank, bow southeast, and I went ahead, put the rudder over to starboard. With a right-hand propeller going ahead floats the stern over. When I did that and got her off far enough then I went astern. She went astern and when I got her clear of the bank I took her right around, just one move right around in a big circle and heading up the harbour. Calm then, no wind. And at half past nine the anchor was running on the bottom.

The next morning they had to get a surveyor and the same Captain Murray that I knew well in the CPR, he had retired, he got the job. Twenty-five dollars. [Captain James Murray, once captain of the *Empress of Britain*, had recently arrived as assistant to Admiral Bertram Chambers, the convoy commander who had himself just come from Britain mid-November.] Everything was working in my favour. After the survey, the wind that had been NNE and dragged that ship ashore

White Star ocean liner RMS *Olympic*, sister ship to *Titanic*, served through the First World War as a troop carrier known as "Old Reliable." NOVA SCOTIA ARCHIVES

had swung around to WNW, blowing a gale. I asked Holloway when had the *Olympic* left New York. "Well, she hasn't left yet, but she will be leaving I think in an hour or two."

"Well," I said, "There's a fair chance I can get her coal."

I went down. The WNW wind blew the ice off Louisbourg. I crept in, got the coal aboard and by that time the ice was drifting down off Ingonish. Coming along further the ice had blown farther offshore. We came around the rocks at Gull Island and headed for Halifax. When I was coming around Devil's Island the *Olympic* was coming by Sambro. There wasn't a pound of coal in Halifax because they were snowed up, all the mines, the province and all. The captain blew his whistle to me, he saw his coal coming alongside. That was a close shave.

The close shave Mackey would attempt to avoid just a few days later did not turn out quite so happily. *Olympic*, full of coal and crammed with Chinese coolies going to work for the war effort, got safely away before the explosion

Memorial for Captain James Murray, discovered in a Quebec City cathedral.

on December 6, but several other ships in the harbour would be damaged or sunk with the loss of many lives. Captain James Murray, who had inspected *Sarah Radcliffe* and sent her expeditiously off to Louisbourg, appeared on the tug *Hilford* alongside Mackey's lifeboat amid the chaos just after the collision that fateful morning. Mackey thought Murray didn't hear his shouted warning, but as a high-ranking officer Murray probably knew what *Mont Blanc* was carrying and realized the situation was dire. The tug hurried Captain James Murray over to a dock where he tried to call the convoy office, but the blast killed him instantly.

Chapter 2

COLLISION COURSE

The explosion that killed Captain Murray and thousands of others in Halifax on the morning of December 6, 1917, followed the collision of an outgoing steamer, *Imo*, with a heavily laden munitions ship, *Mont Blanc*. Francis Mackey, by chance, was the pilot assigned to guide *Mont Blanc* into Bedford Basin. Though he seldom mentioned it to other members of his family, Mackey felt free to speak openly with his son-in-law about that awful accident. He told Ed how the tragedy was set in motion on the first of December in New York.

Mackey had learned from his conversations with *Mont Blanc*'s skipper, Captain Aimé LeMédec, that the British Admiralty had ordered this old French steamer to be loaded with a terrible cargo of explosives at Gravesend Bay, on the east side of New York Harbor. That mixture of TNT, gun cotton, and picric acid was so dangerous the dockworkers had to cover their boots with cloth so as not to strike sparks. Then barrels of benzol were tied onto the decks. The ship was too slow for the convoy leaving New York for the war in Europe, so *Mont Blanc* was ordered to head for Bedford Basin and try for a convoy there. The French skipper had sealed orders he was meant to open if he couldn't hook up with a slow convoy and had to cross the Atlantic alone. Francis Mackey would unfortunately come to have a brief, intense acquaintance with LeMédec on the afternoon of December 5, 1917, and the morning after.

Mackey described to Ed how *Mont Blanc* came crawling up the coast of Nova Scotia and met a bad storm on the way. It had taken the French steamer five or six days to get this far. So when the unlucky old boat arrived off Halifax on the afternoon of December 5, it happened that Captain Mackey had just taken out one ship, *Kentucky*, and bringing in *Mont Blanc* was his next assignment. No rest was possible. Mackey was the senior pilot, and there were only about a dozen others, working plenty of overtime with the convoys and all the other wartime harbour traffic.

It was too late that evening for ships to enter the harbour as the submarine nets were closed to prevent U-boat attacks. *Mont Blanc* would have to anchor off McNabs Island for the night. By then Mackey was aware of what kind of dangerous cargo the ship was carrying. Even so, the pilot decided to stay on board to get an early start in the morning. It was only recently that the convoy system had begun to operate out of Bedford Basin, where merchant ships gathered while waiting to sail in a group across the Atlantic. Escorted by a few British naval vessels, they hoped for a safer voyage through U-boat-infested waters. So far there were no restrictions on what sorts of vessels could enter the harbour to join a convoy. The war must go on, said the government far away in Ottawa.

The pilot's familiar story would unfold for Ed, who maintained a patient interest, and later for CBC Radio's Bob Cadman, who interviewed Mackey in 1958: "So I got aboard the *Mont Blanc* and the man from the examining boat came alongside, as they all had to do to find out what the ship's cargo was and so on, in connection with sailing up to Bedford Basin. First he thought to do me a good turn by getting word from the forts to allow me to pass up, but it was too late for him to do that. I would have been breaking the law and so would he. I

Submarine nets blocking the main entrance to Halifax Harbour. FROM THE COLLECTION OF THE MARITIME MUSEUM OF THE ATLANTIC, HALIFAX, NOVA SCOTIA.

wouldn't attempt it. A fine afternoon." But Mackey did ask that special arrangements be made for safe passage the next morning, now that he knew the nature of the hazards above and below the decks.

The examining officer who came aboard *Mont Blanc* that afternoon was Mate Terrence Freeman, RNCVR; he was surprised to discover a full cargo of explosives. Apparently he had no particular instructions covering such a situation, and the port's federal traffic regulations had no special procedure in place for dealing with munitions ships. As naval historian John Griffith Armstrong observes, "Freeman had no prerogative to treat the arrival of *Mont Blanc* as other than routine."

On December 5 Mackey spent a quiet evening chatting with LeMédec, who told the pilot with regret that no liquor was allowed on board and there was definitely to be no smoking. It was the first time LeMédec had commanded this particular vessel and he was deeply concerned about its ability to keep up with a convoy. The prospect of crossing the Atlantic alone, without protection against prowling U-boats and on top of such a volatile mix of explosives, must have made for anxious nights in LeMédec's passage from New York, but Francis Mackey told Ed he himself slept well that night, the sleep of an overworked and weary pilot.

Next morning at daylight, the examining boat came to order *Mont Blanc* to get under way. The pilot asked if there were any special orders in the way of protection for this unusually dangerous ship. "No sir, just proceed as usual," came the response. But as Mackey soon discovered, proceeding as usual would not be possible that day.

The Norwegian vessel *Imo*, which was supposed to have left port the day before, was delayed because the coal boat had not arrived in time. *Imo* was assigned to the Belgian relief operation and was headed for New York to pick up essential supplies for delivery to civilians in the war zone; her mission, BELGIAN RELIEF, was clearly designated in large letters on her hull to discourage attacks. So on the morning of December 6, *Imo*, anxious to make up for lost time, came thundering out of Bedford Basin and seemed intent on claiming the Dartmouth side of the harbour.

When it became apparent that *Imo* was unwilling or unable to change course and pass properly, port to port, Mackey and the French captain ordered *Mont Blanc* toward the centre of the harbour, across *Imo*'s bow. For a few moments it

Stern of *Mont Blanc* on a happier visit to Halifax in August 1900. FROM THE COLLECTION OF THE MARITIME MUSEUM OF THE ATLANTIC, HALIFAX, NOVA SCOTIA.

appeared the two vessels were parallel and could pass safely, starboard to starboard. But suddenly *Imo* went astern, a move that swung her bow directly toward *Mont Blanc*. A collision was now impossible to avoid. The Norwegian vessel sliced deep into the munitions ship's forward hold filled with picric acid, then pulled back, metal rasping against metal. Sparks and intense fire followed, with a massive explosion about twenty minutes later, thanks to the outrageous combination of munitions on board *Mont Blanc*.

That devil's brew had been placed there on orders from the British Admiralty and by no fault of Mackey's. Nor was he to blame for issues with the control of harbour traffic. Ever since the war began, local officials had been requesting help from the federal government to add more pilots and boats and to clarify who was in charge; sadly, the same problems continued even after the explosion: the *Ottawa Evening Journal* of January 25, 1918, raised the crucial question again: "Has everything been done that expert organizers can devise to prevent a recurrence of the December 6 horror? Well, 'special regulations' have been put in force by the port administration, and they have 'drafted' another set of rules, presumably still more strict or automatic. Drafted, be it observed, but NOT in effect. They were sent to Ottawa two weeks ago for approval, which has NOT YET been given."

Mackey never had reason to doubt his own competence and judgment, and was certain he had made the correct and in fact *only* possible decision to avoid a head-on collision with *Imo*; facing this kind of imminent danger, international rules allow that such a normally forbidden move is justified. In his detailed 1958 interview for CBC Radio, only six minutes of which were made public, Mackey described what was still so vivid in his memory forty years later.

> We came up, arrived at the Narrows. We were coming up as slow as we possibly could, just steerage way on her. And the other ship was coming down on his wrong side, answering my one blast with two, decidedly opposite to what he should do. He should have answered me with one and kept close to the Halifax side. Now then, every blast I blew was answered by him with two. I kept my side. My starboard side was along by the French Cable Wharf and the brewery there, and I couldn't steer any closer without putting her ashore.

Frank Mackey and William Hayes were good friends and had worked together as harbour pilots for two decades. In fact they had gone up to Bedford Basin on the same Pickford and Black boat the afternoon before, but since it turned out *Imo* couldn't leave the evening of December 5, Hayes went home for the night. Many years later Mackey explained to the CBC interviewer how it might have happened that Wyatt, the chief examining officer, didn't know that *Imo* had not left for New York on schedule.

> The Pickford and Black boat picked Hayes up in the Basin to bring him down, and he thought, I suppose, they were going to land him at the dockyard where the Chief Examining Officer's office was, on board *Niobe*. But they took him right down to Pickford and Black's wharf. He said, "I'll have to go back to the *Niobe* to report the ship didn't go out, the *Imo*." Well, the sad part of it was, they said, "You go home, we'll look after that." Now the man's dead.

Hayes went home, and they tried to get the fellow in the *Niobe*'s office, and Wyatt, the CXO, was ashore to a wedding party and the theatre that night. Of course he left his sub there but they couldn't get him all night.

Apparently William Hayes returned to *Imo* early the next morning, but what actually happened on the bridge of that ship will never be known, since both captain and pilot were killed. *Imo* blew ashore on the Dartmouth side when *Mont Blanc* exploded, scattering fragments and huge chunks of metal for kilometres. None of *Imo*'s surviving crew could shed any light on the strange signals and actions of the officers on deck.

Often, Ed heard the Captain say that when *Imo* kept blowing two blasts, meaning the pilot wanted to keep to the Dartmouth shore, leaving *Mont Blanc* no room at all, he was puzzled. "'I knew that pilot well,' he would tell me. 'I was pretty sure that somebody else must have given that signal. Hayes would never have done that.'" The newspapers highlighted that possibility right after the explosion, with headlines suggesting someone other than Pilot Hayes had guided *Imo* that morning. There were anxious rumours spreading around the city about German spies, but they turned out to be baseless.

Captain Mackey believed it was more likely that the Norwegian skipper was in a big rush to get out of Halifax since he was behind schedule, and perhaps he took control of *Imo* away from the pilot in order to go quite a lot faster than harbour rules allowed. "He was a hothead, that Captain From. He was in trouble in the States for trying to leave port without paying for repairs to his ship. My lawyers found that out," Captain Mackey told Ed, who offered the theory to me. Mona agreed, "I heard Father say he thought there was somebody on that ship with a gun on William Hayes's back."

During the 1958 CBC interview, Mackey was still not convinced his friend William Hayes could have made such a tragic mistake:

> The question is whether or not the captain took her out of the pilot's hands, which could have been. He was an erratic sort of fellow, the captain of the *Imo*. Knowing Hayes as I did, it seemed to me that was not his signal. The *Imo* had passed a ship on the wrong side up above

the Narrows and he kept going toward Tufts Cove way. When he got down a little farther he found it was narrowing up across him and he got cold feet and put it full speed astern when he was on my starboard side, and that's what cut her into me.

They tried to make out I was on the Halifax side but that was decidedly wrong because the ship drifted over there after he struck it. The friction between the plates of the two ships created a spark. The benzol was on deck and some of it might have seeped down there and just contacted that little spark.

We stood there as long as we could, the fire on the deck, until it was no use to stay there any longer. I said to the captain, "I was always taught as a seaman in a case of wreckage, a wreck happening, or any danger (of course I was referring to rocks because that's what the rule was taken from), the only thing to do is save your crew. Our ship is out of business, no chance of doing anything with her. Get 'em in the boats! Get 'em in the boats!"

Within a few days of the collision, Captain Aimé LeMédec recorded his version of events through a translator, probably directed or approved by Emile Gaboury, the French consul in Halifax.

It was a clear morning. The water was smooth and we were proceeding at half speed on the starboard side, toward the Bedford Basin. There were no vessels in our course until we sighted the Belgian relief ship *Imo*, coming out of Bedford Basin and headed for the Dartmouth shore. She was more than two miles away at this time. We signalled we would keep the *Mont Blanc* to the starboard going up to the basin, where we were to anchor and await convoy. We headed a little more inshore so as to make clear to the *Imo* our purpose. She signalled that she was coming down on the port, which would bring her on the same side with us. We were keeping to our right, or starboard, according to pilotage rules, and could not understand what the *Imo* meant. But we kept on our course, hoping that she would come down, as she should, on the starboard side, which would keep her on the Halifax side of the harbour and the *Mont Blanc* on the Dartmouth side.

But to our surprise the *Imo* kept coming down on the port side, so we signalled again. We saw there was danger of collision and signalled to stop the engines at the same time veering slightly to port, which brought the two vessels with starboards parallel when about three hundred feet apart.

Then we put the rudder hard to port to try to pass the *Imo* before she should come on us and at the same time the *Imo* reversed engines. As she was light and without cargo, the reverse brought her around now pointing toward our starboard and as a collision was then inevitable, we held the *Mont Blanc* so she would be struck at the forward hold, where the picric acid was, a substance which would not explode, rather than have her strike us where the T.N.T. was stored.

We were in the Narrows, where the harbour is about three-quarters of a mile wide. The *Imo* cut into us about a third through the deck and hold and the benzol poured into the picric acid, igniting it and causing a cloud of smoke to rise from the vessel forward. I saw there was no hope of doing anything more and knew that an explosion was inevitable, so the boats were lowered and all hands got aboard them and rowed for the Dartmouth shore. Pilot Mackey went with us.

In all there were 41 men aboard the *Mont Blanc*. She was headed at the time for the Halifax shore and toward Pier 8. She was making very little headway, as we had to push the boat away from the side. This was about twenty minutes before the explosion but the picric acid was in fumes.

In the meantime the *Imo* had backed away toward the Dartmouth shore. We landed and ran into the woods. About twenty minutes after we left the ship we heard the explosion. It knocked every one of us down and we were struck by steel and other things, but only the gunner was seriously injured. He has died.

The first officer Jean Glotin makes practically the same statement. Both statements make clear the fact that something was wrong on the *Imo*. Although she had on board Pilot Hayes, considered one of the best pilots in Halifax.

This statement was published in the December 10, 1917, edition of the *Boston Herald* and several other newspapers. It was strange for *Mont Blanc*'s skipper to make a public statement before the official inquiry began, but the French consul likely hoped to quell the growing anger toward Captain LeMédec and Pilot Mackey.

There was no panic aboard *Mont Blanc*, as far as Pilot Mackey could see. The crew remained at their posts until they got the order to lower the lifeboats. At that point one observer on a nearby ship claimed he saw sailors "scrambling like rats" down the ladders—and no wonder! There was no way to fight the fire or get at the anchor or open the seacocks, and they knew very well what cargo they carried. Captain LeMédec, swayed by tradition, at first refused to leave his ship, but Mackey persuaded him that this would be a senseless sacrifice and slid down with him to the second lifeboat.

At Mackey's direction they rowed for the Dartmouth shore, and despite the crew's lack of English they tried to warn other boats moving toward the fire, including Captain Murray's tug *Hilford*. "Hollered, but you might as well holler at the moon. Nobody could hear, too much racket," Mackey told Ed many years later, still hurt by the blame laid on him for saving his own life and supposedly failing to warn others of the danger. "As it turned out it was still about twenty minutes before the whole thing went up, but who would know?" Ed observed ruefully. "All those second-guessers who said the pilot should have gone astern sooner didn't know what he had been warned about the cargo. If he had reversed *Mont Blanc* that close to the Dartmouth shore they would certainly have hit bottom, and that could have finished it in a flash."

One of the "second-guessers" Ed chastised was the owner of the *Halifax Herald*, Senator Dennis, a powerful Conservative supporter of Prime Minister Robert Borden. In addition to the *Herald*'s frequent angry headlines attacking Pilot Mackey, Dennis published this editorial on December 29, 1917:

> It would be an appropriate question to ask Pilot Mackey why HE did not see that the explosives flag, the red, was kept flying at the masthead.

He knew the character of the cargo, though the dockyard officials apparently did not, else they would have escaped for their lives when they saw the fire. But Mackey knew it. He knew, or was told, that even a rough jolt against a pier could blow the whole thing up.

Another thing: when Pilot Mackey saw the ship to be on fire, or immediately after the collision, why did he not head her up towards Bedford Basin where she could explode with less danger to the city? The damage would have been confined largely to the ships at anchor there, and the city as a whole would have been saved. As it was, the damage to shipping in the harbour was no less serious than it would have been in the Basin.

The Pilot could have turned the ship into the Basin and allowed the crew to jump for their lives in the Narrows, which they could well have done. He could have stuck to the ship til he got her well up into the Basin. There was time enough; and then he could have escaped himself. That would have been an act of heroism and would have made Pilot Mackey glorious.

Senator Dennis apparently did not know the wartime rules: the red-flag signal was used only when offloading munitions and was otherwise not displayed, so as not to provide useful information to the enemy. Dennis of course had the advantage of hindsight in giving his instructions about what action the pilot should have taken; nobody on *Mont Blanc* could have known whether there would be twenty minutes or twenty seconds before the blast. "The only thing to do was to get on the beach, turn the men ashore," Mackey explained to the CBC.

The Captain was driving his men and I went up on the bank, looking at the thing, expecting her to go off any time and the Captain came and put a hand on my shoulder. "Come on, come on!" So we both turned around to run and we didn't get any distance. Just as quick as that we were knocked down.

I had a raincoat on here and it was taken off the same as if you had a rusty knife and cut it right around the waist. We were knocked right down and a tree fell over us, just like a miracle. The branches on it were

Near the lifeboats' landing spot, the Oland Brewery was probably the first shocking sight when Pilot Mackey recovered consciousness. NOVA SCOTIA ARCHIVES

bigger than my arm. I guess I must have been down there probably ten or fifteen minutes. I was smelling this stuff, I knew I was alive and after a while I stood up.

This much later account echoed the testimony Mackey had given at the Wreck Commissioner's Inquiry in 1917: "I waved the lifeboats toward Dartmouth, I thought they could get there faster and it was the opposite way of the ship, and there were trees on the other side. I was knocked down and stunned. I felt I was kicking the ground and everything was darkness, and I found the Captain close to me and we had just been getting out from under a tree torn out by the roots."

After the horrific blast Captain LeMédec and the French crew were gathered and secured on board the HMS *Highflyer*, in part for questioning but also for their own safety. (Anti-French sentiment was plentiful in Halifax at the time because Quebec had opposed conscription.) Later that day Captain Walter Hose, suddenly in charge because of other officers' injuries, brought *Mont Blanc* crew members to the dockyard where he asked Mr. Townshend, a staff member who had spent the day dispensing blankets and beds and food from the victualing stores, to escort these refugees to the French Consulate.

If it had been possible to see through the smoke, Mackey might have been witness to scenes like this: damaged Roome Street school still standing, but more than eighty children killed in the houses and streets leading up to it. Nova Scotia Archives

On his walk toward the ferry, Mackey would have passed by the Norwegian vessel *Imo*, blown ashore by the blast. Nova Scotia Archives

Even after so much time had passed, Francis Mackey still captured in his 1958 interview the shock that must have overcome his senses. The magnitude of what had just happened was beyond understanding.

> There was fire on the Halifax side, everywhere smoke, some of that stuff was all over me. I was black as could be. I started then to walk down towards the ferry, quite a distance down. Cool when I got down there, buildings smashed in. I saw a man that I knew before. He was a druggist. I said hello. I said, "I was looking around here to see if there was any place I can get a cap." There were no shops, all smashed in… and he says, "Here's mine" and gave me his cap, a new one too it happened to be. I came across on the ferry and went in the pilot office first.

Mackey had apparently been left to his own devices. Unconscious for perhaps fifteen or twenty minutes, he might well have been in shock for some time, as indeed were many survivors that day and for weeks thereafter. Yet his deliberate

The Pilotage Commission office in 1917 was just uphill from the ferry terminal at 70 Bedford Row, second building from the corner. Nova Scotia Archives

actions on December 6 were reflective of his strong, stoic character, an impression that would be reinforced by his performance on the witness stand a week later. It was a warm cap he needed, not sympathy. Duty required that he report to the pilotage office before searching for his family.

By mid-morning, alarm had spread about a possible second explosion as flames approached dockyard munitions. As he trudged from the waterfront toward his Robie Street house, through streets filled with broken glass and terribly injured people seeking help, Francis Mackey must have wondered what he would find there. There is no record of his thoughts as he walked through the chaos. But he had certainly seen the flames and smoke across the harbour when his consciousness returned.

Mona, not yet four the day of the explosion, still remembered in her nineties the sound of every window in their house shattering. Most of her siblings were at school when the explosion happened but they somehow made it back home. She still had a vivid image of her oldest sister, Florence, the only one of the Mackey children physically injured that day:

> She had glass blown into her face and her chest at St. Patrick's girls' school down on Brunswick Street. They said one of the sisters pulled a big sharp piece out from the apex of her heart, probably saved her life. I do remember that I saw her walking along the upstairs hall. She was wearing what they called in those days a singlet, shirt and pants all in one, and I remember seeing blood there. Florence always had the marks on her face, little scars with a tinge of blue.

Marjorie, the middle sister, was at the College Street School that morning, Mona recalled. Although a cupboard fell right beside her, she was not hurt. The boys, Ronnie and Gerald, were lucky too, and the youngest brother, Douglas, would not be born until eight months later.

When rumours of an impending second explosion spread through the city that awful morning, soldiers came around ordering Mona and her family out of their house. "Mother and our servant girl got us dressed and out to the field at Camp Hill," she explained. She was not afraid while they waited in the open field, shivering more from excitement than chill, because her mother kept them together and sang to them. As an adult, she realized her mother must have been desperately anxious about what might have happened to her husband out there on the harbour, while she worried too about how to protect her children against unknown perils.

Strange to tell, Gertrude Hayes and her three children had been forced out to the Commons also, and might well have been nearby. Agnes Hayes, just the same age as Mona, later told her children about sitting on a little chest that she believed contained all Pilot Hayes's money. There was another younger sister and the baby, Charles, just eight months old. (He would later become the lifelong friend of the youngest Mackey, Douglas.) They were all too young to take in what had happened to their father, or to recall when the bad news reached Mrs. Hayes.

What a relief when Captain Mackey appeared! The Mackey family's maid, Lizzie Brooks, ran to tell him that his wife and children were safe, and at last they were able to go home. But first, Francis Mackey had to assume the voice of authority and take command of the situation.

So I got to the house. There was a soldier outside saying, "Not allowed in!" Well I said, "I'm going in, I own this house!" We had a hall stove and it wasn't upset but the porch was all smashed in. The stove out in the kitchen was all right but all the storm windows, nineteen altogether, they hadn't been put on. Good that they weren't! So I got a fire on, got some hot tea and got after them. I got all those storm windows on at half past nine and I was ready to lie down. Swept up glass the last thing 'til three o'clock in the morning, and that was that.

To find his house standing, though damaged, and his family alive must have eased Mackey's worst fears. But he left us only the account of a practical man dealing with another challenge on a busy day. As soon as the harbour was cleared of debris, he was back on pilot duty with the first convoys ready to leave five days later.

The kind of courage required to return so soon to the deck of a ship, not knowing what might be under that deck, or what changes might have been made to the sea floor and reefs and harbour depth by the explosion and the tsunami that followed, is not often found in mere mortals. But pilots were a different breed, accustomed to risk and danger as they transferred daily from small rowboats to swinging rope ladders in all sorts of weather, up the side of whatever heaving ship needed their guidance and local knowledge. Pilot Mackey had all of that courage and more, and he was about to need it on a different kind of voyage, as he headed into the uncharted reefs and whirlpools of the legal turmoil that lay ahead.

Chapter 3

WHO IS TO BLAME?

Mont Blanc blew up with a force greater than humans had ever created before, and the damage was appalling. Richmond, the area closest to the harbour, was obliterated in seconds. Houses toppled, trapping people inside, while their overturned stoves started fires that swept through entire streets. Whole families vanished: two thousand dead (probably more since it is likely that some bodies were never recovered from collapsed factories and schools, and others may have been swept away by the ensuing tidal wave) and twelve thousand injured, many blinded by flying glass. Twenty thousand were left homeless, the railway lines, station, and port facilities destroyed, ships mangled or sunk, and windows shattered everywhere in the rest of the city.

Archibald MacMechan, appointed by the Executive Committee of the Halifax Relief Commission to record the explosion's scenes, undertook the task with determination, but his vivid descriptions stayed hidden in the Dalhousie University archives until 1978, when they were published in Graham Metson's book, *The Halifax Explosion December 6 1917.*

> Under the wreckage of Richmond that morning there were hundreds of human beings injured, but in some cases unhurt, who were to die by fire. The mind refuses to dwell upon the horrors of that morning, men and women like ourselves, broken, bruised, bleeding, half-conscious or worse still, uninjured but imprisoned in the wreckage and the inexorable flames coming swiftly nearer. The pity of it...to see your own

perish in torment before your eyes and being impotent to help. All that morning a tall silvery column of smoke rose to the sky above the burning North End…the streets were filled with the strangest apparitions: men, women and children with their faces streaming with blood from wounds dealt by flying glass, faces chalk-white with terror and streaked with red, faces black with the "black rain" and smeared with blood. The dead, the dying and the severely injured lay about the streets, amid ghastly fragments of what had been human being's heads and limbs… Some were dazed and semi-conscious from the shock. Some were uttering shrieks of pain and terror. Some were helping injured people away or trying to extricate them from the ruin of their houses. There was no order or direction.

Soldiers search for bodies in the ruins of the car works, one of several Richmond factories destroyed by the blast. Nova Scotia Archives

Suddenly the devastated city was faced with enormous challenges. Within hours of the explosion, while city council was putting together committees to deal with the immediate emergencies, the Ministry of Marine and Fisheries in Ottawa ordered a full investigation. Since the explosion's cause was a collision between two ships, the Canada Shipping Act decreed the inquiry be undertaken by the much-feared Dominion Wreck Commissioner Louis Demers, an experienced master mariner with a reputation for dealing severely with any seaman found to blame for loss or damage to ships. He was not one to accept excuses or extenuating circumstances, and could be depended upon to deliver punishment in any situation he investigated.

Judge Arthur Drysdale of the Nova Scotia Supreme Court was appointed to preside over the Wreck Commissioner's Inquiry with the assistance of Demers and with Captain Walter Hose, RCN, as naval representative. Alexander Johnston, the deputy minister of Marine, made all of these arrangements with amazing speed; on that same day he appointed Halifax lawyer William Henry KC to act as Crown counsel, and authorized him to detain any potentially useful witnesses. Johnston also ordered the local pilotage authority, the Halifax Pilot Commission, not to undertake any investigative action itself.

Despite the chaos in the city, the severe blizzard and heavy rains in the days following the explosion, and the damage to rail transportation, which delayed the arrival of Demers, the inquiry began the following week, on December 13, 1917. Donald Kerr, lawyer and historian, describes the intimidating scene as "almost Dickensian," stating, "The Inquiry convened in a large room with twenty-five foot ceilings.... The windows had been blown out by the explosion and were boarded up. Power was unavailable and the room was dimly lit with two oil lamps. Drysdale peered down through the gloom from an elevated Victorian pulpit, flanked on either side by the two master mariners who were to serve as his advisors."

There was intense public interest of course, fuelled by the local press. Immediately after the explosion the *Halifax Herald* headlined the hope that the court of inquiry would reveal who was to blame for the tragedy and the wreckage left behind. But that revelation never did come about in a way that would bring closure or relief. The *Herald* began its campaign of provocative criticism on December 12, with the headline SOME ONE BLUNDERED - WHO? COURT MAY DECIDE. The Halifax *Morning Chronicle* of December 11, meanwhile, had expressed hope that the inquiry would bring out "the whole truth about the cause of a catastrophe which in its burden of tragedy and sorrow has probably never been paralleled in history."

Because he was confident he had done the right thing while guiding *Mont Blanc* that fateful morning, Francis Mackey went willingly before the Wreck Commissioner's Inquiry on December 15, 1917. On his first day of testimony Mackey believed that the inquiry's purpose was to learn what in fact had happened on the harbour. He described the challenge he faced as *Imo*, with foam at her bow indicating she was moving well above the harbour speed limit, kept blowing two blasts to claim the channel on the Dartmouth shore instead of steering toward the proper Halifax side.

Mackey remained on the stand for three days, much longer than any other witness, and was grilled without mercy by Charles Burchell, lawyer for *Imo's* owners, the Southern Pacific Whaling Company. Humphrey Mellish much more politely represented La Compagnie Générale Transatlantique, owners of *Mont Blanc.* But immediately the inquiry became a struggle between lawyers for the two shipping companies, both seeking to escape responsibility, rather than a fact-finding exercise.

The blame-the-pilot theme was blatantly evident, and charges without foundation were quickly reported in the press as if proven. The December 15, 1917, *Morning Chronicle* carried a headline that was not at all supported in the story it advertized, but was certainly provocative: WITNESSES SAY MONT BLANC WAS GOING FASTER THAN THE STEAMER IMO. Subtitles were equally slanted: COMMENTED THAT "THEY APPEARED TO BE VERY NERVOUS ON THE *MONT BLANC*"; STEERING ORDERS GIVEN IN ENGLISH TO MEMBERS OF A FRENCH CREW, THE PILOT'S FRENCH.

Despite the fact that Aimé LeMédec was reasonably capable in English, and despite the sworn agreement of both the French captain and Pilot Mackey that they communicated perfectly with hand signals, lawyer Charles Burchell was quick to seize the opportunity to discredit and mock the pilot. The *Morning Chronicle* assisted Burchell, with this December 17 report:

> Pilot Mackey had given the French for "port" and "starboard" and Mr. Burchell seeking further information had asked the witness how he would say "half-speed" in French. There was considerable laughter in

the court when Pilot Mackey replied "demi tasse." Mr. Burchell yesterday afternoon asked the signalman what he would do if the words "demi tasse" were spoken to him as an order, and witness replied that he supposed he would have gone down below and procured a cup of coffee.

Archibald MacMechan, appointed official historian, compiled *The Halifax Disaster* in a room rented at the office of the *Morning Chronicle*, so it is not surprising he repeated that story and, without awaiting the results of the inquiry, condemned Mackey and *Mont Blanc*: "At the last moment the MONT BLANC turned out of her course, directly across the bows of the IMO. Why she did so can perhaps never be known. One plausible theory is that the pilot's order at the critical moment was misunderstood, owing to the difference between the French and English words of command."

Even more hostile than the *Morning Chronicle*, the *Halifax Herald* set its pattern of sensational reportage casting suspicion on Pilot Mackey with its front-page headline on December 17: MONT BLANC WAS EXCEEDING THE SPEED LIMIT, it trumpeted, despite contradicting that assertion in the first paragraph; the reporter immediately shifted that message to reflect what Mackey had actually testified: "The Imo when first sighted, was carrying white foam at her bow and exceeding the speed limit set by the Admiralty." Typically misleading were these headlines from the December 18 *Herald*: BURCHELL ACCUSES PILOT OF FAILING TO WARN OTHERS; WAS PILOT MACKEY JUSTIFIED IN STARBOARDING THE MONT BLANC'S HELM?; PILOT MACKEY ADMITS IN GRUELLING CROSS EXAMINATION THAT HE KNEW THE NATURE OF MONT BLANC'S CARGO. The word "admits" unfairly implies that Mackey had previously lied in response to the question. The papers never failed to publish the lawyer's charges but seldom included the pilot's responses, and public fury toward him grew with every unproven allegation.

In his 1958 CBC interview Francis Mackey offered his appraisal of what happened during the inquiry:

> Now when it went to court they did their damnedest to try to fasten
> it on the pilots, if they could, and the pilot commission, to try to find a

goat to save the guilty ones! We had good men in the dockyard too you know, they weren't all bad; there were some that were sent out from England that knew what they were doing, and the transport officer at that time, his name was Holloway, was a very fine man and he knew his business. I was doing the CPR there for eight years between Saint John and Halifax, and the Royal Mail and Steam Packet Company, and before this explosion I was doing jobs right and left for the dock-yard, for the transport officer.

Evidently Pilot Mackey had a long record of excellent service and a professional relationship with the shipping authorities. That history, as well as his firm belief that he had done exactly what was necessary on the morning of the explosion, allowed Mackey to remain calm and controlled on the stand despite all the abuse and attempts at entrapment hurled in his direction.

There had been no opportunity for Mackey to confer with LeMédec, yet the pilot's version of events substantially supported that of *Mont Blanc*'s captain. Their accounts were noted by Crown Counsel William Henry, and even later by the Privy Council in London, as reliable and consistent with each other and with the testimony of those witnesses in the best positions to see the collision clearly. There were, however, many conflicting reports from those who may have seen the event from a different vantage point, and Judge Drysdale quickly accepted whatever testimony supported his preordained decision: Mackey and *Mont Blanc* were to blame.

The harbour pilot, however, at first had no idea he was about to become the prime suspect, and he simply stated what he believed to be the truth. On December 16, 1917, Francis Mackey was definite in his testimony, under questioning by Humphrey Mellish, that *Imo* was travelling much faster than was safe or legal:

MACKEY: Seeing him going at that rate of speed, I knew if I kept on he would bang me ashore. I was not in a position to let the anchor go owing to a little flood tide that would swing my ship crosswise in the channel, either out in the channel or swinging her stern ashore, and having on a load of explosives I didn't want to put her ashore. And if I had reversed my engines I knew she would slew ashore, so I decided to give this second blast so as to attract his attention and see if he thought he was making a mistake.

When we were approaching I saw he was going pretty fast. I saw it was no use in keeping to my shore without going ashore and him banging me up on the bank. I decided to starboard my helm and gave him two blasts, and if he had kept on, and I had continued, or been allowed to continue on, I could have improved the position I gave him, although I made it absolutely safe for him to pass me; I could have improved my position by putting engines full speed ahead.

As it was, I was out in the middle of the channel when suddenly he put his engines astern. At the speed he was going he simply twisted her right in and rammed the ship. He made me think that at the time, on account of his going so fast, he was afraid to pass me on that side for fear he would not be able to stop his ship. He went astern too soon in my estimation.

MELLISH: That was your speculation as to what he was thinking?

MACKEY: The first thought that struck me at that time—knowing Hayes as I do—I said that is not your order. I didn't think it was his order. I didn't think Hayes would do that.

MELLISH: You knew him as a competent pilot?

MACKEY: I knew him well; it seemed to strike me very forcibly that the telegraph was rung by somebody else and without his orders.

The *Herald* followed this day's testimony with another melodramatic headline on December 17: DID ANOTHER HAND THAN PILOT'S DIRECT IMO'S COURSE? But Mackey's composure never wavered. He even felt confident enough to display his wry wit on occasion: asked whether he was sure he knew the harbour's rocks well, he replied, "Well, some of the pebbles I might not know."

Despite the pilot's forthright explanation of the circumstances leading up to the collision, Judge Drysdale stuck to his firm belief that Mackey had violated the rules of the road by crossing the bow of the oncoming ship. Most neutral observers expected *Imo* would be charged for coming down the wrong side of the harbour, but Drysdale insisted that since both the pilot and captain of *Imo* were killed and could not now defend themselves, British Fair Play required that no blame could be attached to them. Recalled Mona, "Judge Drysdale…now that was a name I learned to hate, though I didn't quite know why at the time. 'Drysdale was the fly in the ointment,' I remember my father saying." Mona, so many years later, was clearly distressed at the injustice she remembered too well: "This judge claimed he couldn't blame *Imo* because both the captain and the pilot were dead. The judge said that my father was in the wrong, and should have his license taken away, even though many people saw the other ship was where it should not have been, on the Dartmouth side of the harbour."

Judge Drysdale's obvious bias against Mackey and *Mont Blanc* got plenty of support from the belligerent behavior of lawyer Charles Burchell, who came into the inquiry fired up to defend the owners of *Imo* against any possible damage claims. His fury was likely intensified due to his having just spent several

Judge Arthur Drysdale of the Admiralty Court seemed unfit for conducting the Wreck Commissioner's Inquiry, not a criminal court but rather intended to investigate the accident's circumstances.
Nova Scotia Archives

days assisting the desperate rescue efforts in the ruins of Richmond, the northern area of the city closest to the harbour and most seriously damaged. Recovering burned and mangled children from the wreckage might well have inflamed a raging anger in a man already inclined to passionate speechmaking. These are possible explanations but not excuses for Burchell's performance. He employed highly unethical tactics in his drive to trick Mackey into contradicting himself and admitting to errors. And Judge Drysdale did nothing to stop the bullying, since he had already made up his mind that Mackey was guilty.

The most insidious attempt to label Francis Mackey as heartless villain came on the afternoon of the pilot's second day on the witness stand, December 16, after a long morning of Burchell's unsuccessful efforts to trip him up about the position of *Mont Blanc* when the collision happened.

BURCHELL: You know there were some people killed in the explosion that followed?

MACKEY: Yes.

BURCHELL: And you know there were some thousands severely wounded and injured for life?

MACKEY: Yes.

BURCHELL: Do you know the bells are ringing now for this funeral?

MACKEY: I have not heard them.

BURCHELL: I want to ask you now, knowing that this is the hour for the funeral, if you are willing to admit frankly that you have been deliberately perjuring yourself for the last two days?

MACKEY: No!

BURCHELL: You say that everything you have told us is absolutely true?

MACKEY: To the best of my knowledge. To the best of my ability.

BURCHELL: You say that at this hour?

MACKEY: Yes.

BURCHELL: You say that at THIS hour?

MACKEY: Yes!

BURCHELL: You are considerable of a hard drinker yourself?

MACKEY: No.

BURCHELL: A man who frequently gets drunk?

MACKEY: No.

BURCHELL: Sometimes you get drunk?

MACKEY: Not lately. I have sometimes, a long while ago.

BURCHELL: You drink quite a bit? What is known as a constant drinker?

MACKEY: No, I am not a heavy drinker.

Later that afternoon Thomas R. Robertson, counsel for the pilotage commission, gave Mackey a chance to counteract these insinuations.

> ROBERTSON: There have been some aspersions cast on you as to your habits of sobriety. I would like to ask you.
> MACKEY: I am always very careful with liquor, always have been, and when I am on duty I make it a point never to feel the effects of intoxicating liquor.
> ROBERTSON: From the time of going on board the *Mont Blanc* until the time of the collision, at the risk of repeating a question, did you have any intoxicating liquor of any sort? Drink any?
> MACKEY: None at all.

Shortly before Christmas the inquiry was adjourned for a month because Judge Drysdale apparently had other important duties. This hiatus left plenty of time for speculation in the press about Mackey's rumoured perjury and drunkenness.

In the Mackey household there was predictably great concern about what was unfolding. Mona sat unseen at the top of the stairs, curious as any four-year-old would be, and listened to the grownups talking below her. Their voices were troubled and worrisome. Ninety years later, her memory of the tension remained powerful. "I was too young to understand about the inquiry but the older children and my mother knew what was happening and they told me some things later about that time. I found out when I got older that the lawyer for *Imo* accused my father of telling lies on the stand, and of being drunk on the job, and then the papers would print all those charges as if they were true." When hearings resumed at the end of January, Sheriff James Hall, who was also chair of the pilotage commission, spoke in Mackey's defence: "I have known him for probably twenty-five or thirty years. We always looked upon him as one of the best pilots, sober, industrious, and attentive to his duties. We never had any reason to complain of his habits. I never saw him take a drink in my life."

Mona also heard from her older siblings about another part of the story that created quite a stir in the press. Since the pilot commission had been instructed by Deputy Minister of Marine Alexander Johnston to take no action during the inquiry, there seemed to be no reason to suspend Mackey from his piloting duties,

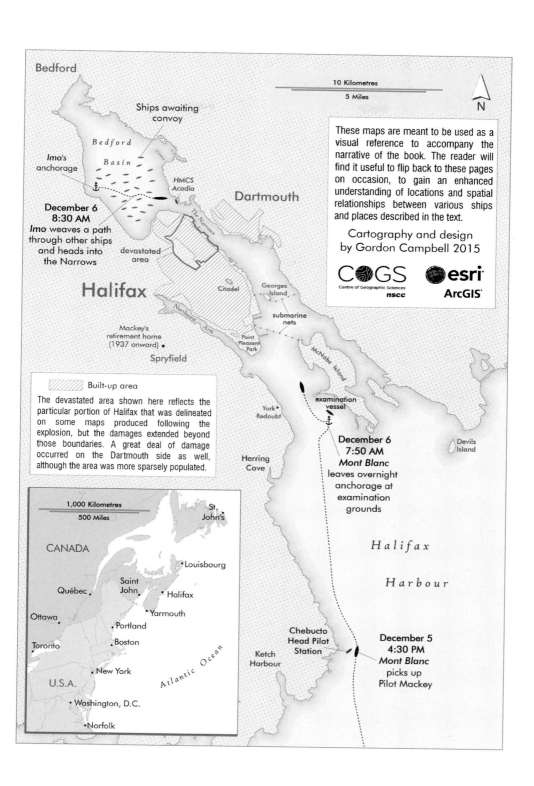

Bedford

10 Kilometres
5 Miles

N

Ships awaiting
convoy

Bedford
Basin

Imo's
anchorage

HMCS
Acadia

Dartmouth

The Narrows

**December 6
8:30 AM**
Imo weaves a path
through other ships
and heads into
the Narrows

devastated
area

Halifax

Northwest Arm

Citadel

Georges
Island

submarine
nets

Mackey's
retirement home
(1937 onward)

Point
Pleasant
Park

Spryfield

McNabs Island

These maps are meant to be used as a
visual reference to accompany the
narrative of the book. The reader will
find it useful to flip back to these pages
on occasion, to gain an enhanced
understanding of locations and spatial
relationships between various ships
and places described in the text.

Cartography and design
by Gordon Campbell 2015

C✺GS
Centre of Geographic Sciences
nscc

⬤esri·
ArcGIS·

///// Built-up area

The devastated area shown here reflects the
particular portion of Halifax that was delineated
on some maps produced following the
explosion, but the damages extended beyond
those boundaries. A great deal of damage
occurred on the Dartmouth side as well,
although the area was more sparsely populated.

York •
Redoubt

examination
vessel

**December 6
7:50 AM**
Mont Blanc
leaves overnight
anchorage at
examination
grounds

Devils
Island

Herring
Cove

Halifax

Harbour

1,000 Kilometres
500 Miles

St.
John's

CANADA

• Louisbourg

Saint
John

Québec •

• Halifax

Ottawa •

• Portland

• Yarmouth

Toronto •

• Boston

Chebucto
Head Pilot
Station

Ketch
Harbour

**December 5
4:30 PM**
Mont Blanc
picks up
Pilot Mackey

• New York

U.S.A.

Atlantic Ocean

• Washington, D.C.

• Norfolk

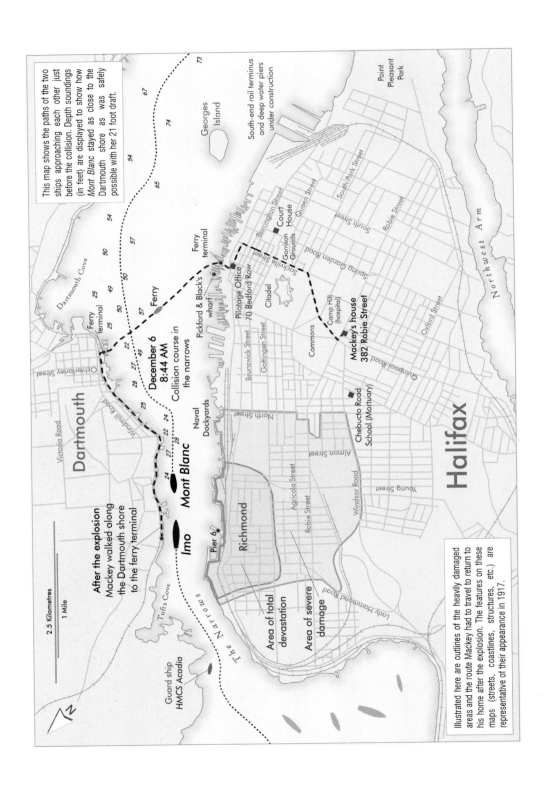

This map shows the paths of the two ships approaching each other just before the collision. Depth soundings (in feet) are displayed to show how close *Mont Blanc* stayed as close to the Dartmouth shore as was safely possible with her 21 foot draft.

2.5 Kilometres
1 Mile

N

Guard ship HMCS Acadia

After the explosion
Mackey walked along the Dartmouth shore to the ferry terminal

Tuft's Cove

The Narrows

Dartmouth Cove

Victoria Road

Windmill Road

Dartmouth

Ferry terminal

Ochterloney Street

73
67
74
54
65
54
54
57
50
49
50
50
57
25
25
50
49
25
22
49
27
28
27
25
24
22
28
27
24

Georges Island

Ferry terminal

Ferry

December 6 8:44 AM
Collision course in the narrows

Imo

Mont Blanc

Pier 6

Naval Dockyards

Richmond

Area of total devastation

Area of severe damage

Lady Hammond Road

South-end rail terminus and deep water piers under construction

Point Pleasant Park

North West Arm

Pickford & Black's wharf

Pilotage Office
70 Bedford Row

Court House

Barrington Street

Sackville Street

Citadel

Garrison Grounds

Commons

Camp Hill (hospital)

Queen Street

South Park Street

Robie Street

Spring Garden Road

Oxford Street

Quinpool Road

**Mackey's house
382 Robie Street**

Brunswick Street

Gottingen Street

North Street

Almon Street

Agricola Street

Robie Street

Windsor Road

Young Street

Chebucto Road School (Mortuary)

Halifax

Illustrated here are outlines of the heavily damaged areas and the route Mackey had to travel to return to his home after the explosion. The features on these maps (streets, coastlines, structures, etc.) are representative of their appearance in 1917.

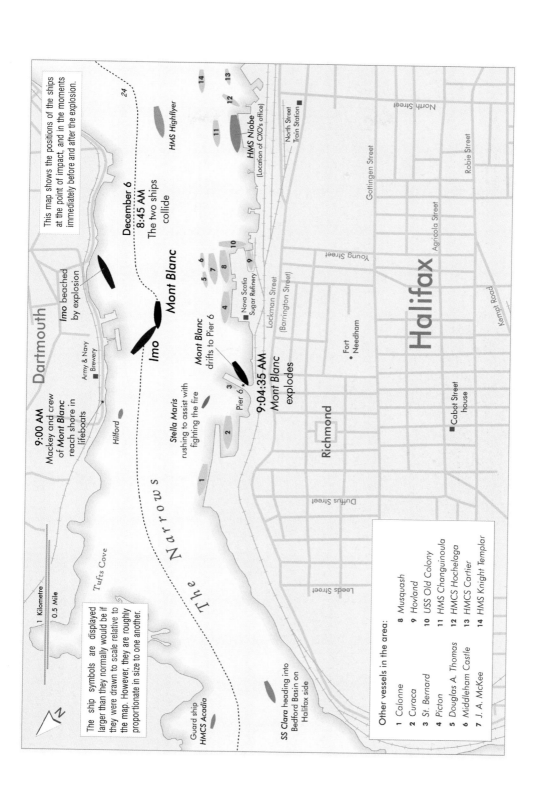

This map shows the positions of the ships at the point of impact, and in the moments immediately before and after the explosion.

Dartmouth

Imo beached by explosion

24

9:00 AM
Mackey and crew of *Mont Blanc* reach shore in lifeboats

Army & Navy
■ Brewery

Hilford

Tufts Cove

1 Kilometre
0.5 Mile

The ship symbols are displayed larger than they normally would be if they were drawn to scale relative to the map. However, they are roughly proportionate in size to one another.

Guard ship
HMCS Acadia

SS Clara heading into Bedford Basin on Halifax side

The Narrows

**December 6
8:45 AM**
The two ships collide

Imo

Mont Blanc

14

13

12

HMS Highflyer

11

HMS Niobe
(Location of CXO's office)

North Street
Train Station ■

North Street

Gottingen Street

Young Street

Agricola Street

Robie Street

Kempt Road

Stella Maris rushing to assist with fighting the fire

Mont Blanc drifts to Pier 6

9:04:35 AM
Mont Blanc explodes

Pier 6

1

2

3

5

7

8

4

6

10

9

Nova Scotia ■ Sugar Refinery

Lockman Street

(Barrington Street)

Richmond

Fort
● Needham

Halifax

■ Cabot Street house

Duffus Street

Leeds Street

Other vessels in the area:

1 Calonne
2 Curaca
3 St. Bernard
4 Picton
5 Douglas A. Thomas
6 Middleham Castle
7 J. A. McKee
8 Musquash
9 Hovland
10 USS Old Colony
11 HMS Changuinoula
12 HMCS Hochelaga
13 HMCS Cartier
14 HMS Knight Templar

Ed and Mona Holmes (2007), still happy to share stories of their seventy years together.

Their daughters: Janet Holmes Connolly spending Christmas 2012 with her father, ninety-eight.

Carole Holmes-Lauder crowns her mother queen on her ninety-fifth birthday.

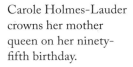

Rita Simmons marries Gerard Dobson, stepson of Pilot Mackey,
attended by the pilot's children, Ronald and Mona Mackey.

ABOVE Debris cleared away, five days after the explosion Francis Mackey was assigned to pilot the first convoy leaving Bedford Basin. ARTHUR LISMER, *CONVOY AT NIGHT, C.1917*. COURTESY OF THE ART GALLERY OF NOVA SCOTIA. PHOTOGRAPH BY STEVE FARMER PHOTOGRAPHY. PERMISSION GRANTED BY JANET CAUFFIEL.

TOP LEFT Photograph revealing the stark ruins of Richmond the day after the explosion. NOVA SCOTIA ARCHIVES

BOTTOM LEFT Halifax-born artist Judy Csukly captured this same scene powerfully: the shattered trees, blizzard's snow covering the wreckage of homes where lines of fire are still smouldering, the knowledge that victims are trapped underneath.

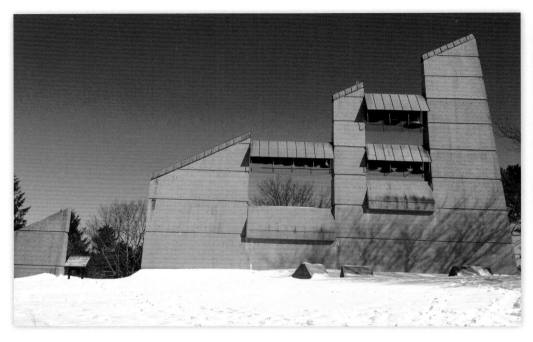

Historian Janet Kitz helped to create this memorial tower on Fort Needham, where bells donated by Barbara Orr (whose whole family died in the explosion) ring the hours. Mrs. Kitz also designed the interpretive panel which points visitors down a path to ground zero, but unfortunately the harbour view is now blocked by a shipbuilding structure.

especially when the need was so great. He had gone out with the first convoy to leave after the harbour was cleared of floating debris. "First of all," Mackey told CBC, "I had to lead out forty-five ships. The man sent out to look after the slow convoy that was held up here on account of the explosion, he knew who I was because he'd had a CPR man [Captain James Murray] working with him that I used to pilot between Saint John and Halifax, the Empresses and other freighters."

James Hall also confirmed to the inquiry that Pilot Mackey was still working in the harbour and had not been suspended, news which was promptly conveyed to a shocked public by the press. "When it came out that my father had still been working as a pilot, at least twenty ships since the explosion, there was a big fuss and they made him stop, even though he had no trouble with any of them," explained Mona. There was a false report circulating that Pilot Mackey had been involved in another near collision since December 6.

Both Hall and Mackey asked to be recalled to the stand in order to testify that there had been no such narrowly avoided disaster. Crown Counsel William Henry asked the pilot, "In that interval between the 6th of December and now, has there been any occasion when it could have been said you were in danger of collision?"

> MACKEY: No sir, I consider it the greatest piece of treachery ever perpetrated.
> HENRY: To say that kind of thing?
> MACKEY: Yes sir.
> HENRY: Your actions since that time have been entirely free of any suspicion of danger?
> MACKEY: Not the slightest sign of it whatever on any occasion.

Once such a damaging rumour is started, however, no one listens to retractions. And so, despite there being no truth in the story, Mackey was suspended. According to Mona, Mackey took his pilot's license to the commission office and hid it behind some books for safekeeping, fully expecting it would be restored once this frustrating inquiry process ended and life got back to normal. As it turned out, that time would be four years away.

Chapter 4

NO VICTORY

B y the time the inquiry ended late in January, there were still more questions than answers. The front page of the January 26, 1918, *Halifax Herald* summarized the ongoing debate:

FURTHER AGONIZING REVELATIONS OF NAVAL, HARBOR AND PILOT MISMANAGEMENT
INEFFICIENCY, BUNGLING AND PIGHEADEDNESS
PILOTS COOLLY IGNORE THE ORDERS OF THE NAVAL AUTHORITIES

The evidence showed the blame to be distributed between the pilots and the naval authorities in this port. THE SUPREME AUTHORITY, resting as it did, and does, in the hands of the naval authorities, does NOT relieve the pilots from responsibilities, but if the supreme authority is not capable of control ITS culpability is the greater.

Over the process of the inquiry, Burchell had been particularly hard on Frank Mackey, accusing him of presenting information that was nothing but conflict and confusion: "I say Pilot Mackey, all through the case, has been that kind of witness. He would say for a minute anything he could see that would help him immediately, acquiesce in any suggestion." Meanwhile, Humphrey Mellish, the lawyer representing *Mont Blanc*, criticized Burchell for the way he harassed Mackey:

From the outset, this pilot has been assailed by counsel for the *Imo*. He has openly and with dramatic intensity, and premeditated insult, been accused of perjury. The bones of the departed have been dragged before him, and the tolling of the funeral bells have been brought to his attention, and he has been charged in the most direct, emphatic and insulting fashion of abusing his conscience and his oath, and I think it is only fair to say that this labouring of the mountain has resulted in the birth of a mouse, and that nothing has come of all these threats that have been made to this pilot.

Despite this passionate defence and despite all evidence to the contrary, Judge Drysdale immediately delivered to Minister of Marine C. C. Ballantyne a brief report condemning Francis Mackey and the French captain of *Mont Blanc* for violating the rules of navigation and for failing to warn the city of the danger; it stated, "Pilot Mackey by reason of his gross negligence should be forthwith dismissed by the Pilotage Authority and his license cancelled." Drysdale strongly recommended criminal prosecution.

Francis Mackey wearing his public face of strength and determination: "I've done nothing wrong."

Warrants had already been prepared and were delivered by Chief of Police Frank Hanrahan. Francis Mackey was arrested and charged with manslaughter as he was leaving the courthouse where the decision was read on February 6, 1918. Sheriff James Hall, who clearly believed Mackey had done no wrong, promptly paid Mackey's bail, set at $6,000. Sadly, Hall's opinion was not a common one on the battered streets of Halifax. Years later, Mona recalled a powerful memory of walking with her father while he was the target of so much anger.

"Murderer! Murderer!" I remember there were men in dark suits on the other side of Barrington Street. I reached for Father's hand but he brushed me off and said, "Just stand up tall and keep walking. I've done nothing wrong and neither did you." That was a message I heard many times again, especially on the sixth of December each year when the newspapers would repeat the old headlines: "Pilot Mackey *Mont Blanc* Explosion Thousands Killed."

On those days Father would go quiet and stay in the End Room, down a few steps from the bedrooms, where his ripped raincoat hung with his fishing gear, and we weren't allowed to talk to him. It must have been hard for him but he never complained. Not to us anyway. But look at this: even in his obituary printed in the *Herald* right after he died on New Year's Eve of 1961, it was right at the top:

"Captain Francis Mackey, pilot of one of the two vessels involved in the 1917 Halifax Explosion, died Sunday at his home in Spryfield. He was 89. Captain Mackey was pilot in change of the French steamer *Mont Blanc* which was in collision Dec 6 with the Norwegian steamer *Imo* in the Halifax Narrows. The *Mont Blanc* carried about 1000 tons of TNT. The resulting explosion killed at least 1,600, injured 6,000 and left 10,000 homeless."

How would you like to be remembered that way? Especially when you know you are not guilty for what happened. People were looking for someone to blame, and the newspapers made him the scapegoat. Likely it was worse because he survived when so many died. He had a lot of courage to get through it.

Prominent pilot dies

Captain Francis Mackey, pilot of one of the two vessels involved in the 1917 Halifax explosion, died Sunday at his home in Spryfield on 5 Mayor Avenue. He was 89.

Captain Mackey was pilot in charge of the French steamer Mont Blanc which was in collision Dec. 6 with the Norwegian steamer Imo in the Halifax Narrows. The Mont Blanc carried about 1,000 tons of TNT.

The resulting explosion killed at least 1,600, injured 6,000 and left 10,000 homeless.

PILOT 45 YEARS

Born in Ketch Harbor, he served 45 years with the pilotage service until retiring in 1937.

Besides his wife Margaret, he is survived by two sons, Ronald, Halifax; Douglas, Beauharnois, Que.; one step-son Gerard Dobson, Halifax; three daughters, Florence (Mrs. W. E. Bryson), Red Deer, Alta.; Mona (Mrs. Edwin J. Holmes), Halifax; and Marjorie, Halifax; two brothers, Samuel and James E., Winnipex; three sisters, Mary Ellen, Victoria; Lucy (Mrs. L. Foster), Winnipeg; Loretta, New York. Sixteen grandchildren and three great-grandchildren also survive.

His first wife and one son Gerald predeceased him.

PAGE SIX

The Halifax Herald
44 Years In The Public Service

WHO IS GUILTY?

WHO IS GUILTY? That question has yet to be answered in connection with the great explosion of December 6.

WHO IS GUILTY? It would seem that no one is to be punished for the criminal carelessness which caused over two thousand deaths, mutilated another three thousand persons, partially or totally blinded hundreds and destroyed three thousand homes.

WHO IS GUILTY? There was no upheaval of nature on that awful day. No enemy sent a shell hurtling into the city. The cause of the disaster was the colliding of two ships, one of which had a cargo of a dangerous combination of the most powerful explosives. No great mystery surrounded the affair and yet it would seem that no one was guilty.

WHO IS GUILTY? This newspaper from the date of the collision urged strongly that a commission be appointed and that a careful investigation be conducted. A commission was appointed, headed by Mr. Justice Drysdale, and for session after session that commission listened to evidence covering every phase of the disaster. The commission reported:
"Such collision was caused by a violation of the rules of navigation.
"That the pilot and master of the steamer Mont Blanc were wholly responsible for violating the rules of the road.
"That Commander Wyatt is guilty of negligence in performing his duty as C.X.O., in not taking proper steps to ensure the regulations being carried out and especially in not keeping himself fully acquainted with the movements and intended movements of vessels in the harbor."

WHO IS GUILTY? The question then was shifted to another court on a charge of manslaughter. Mr. Justice Russell reviewed the evidence which had painstakingly been taken before Mr. Justice Drysdale and after further proceedings announced his opinion that the man who was really guilty had not been located. An all round acquittal has followed and it now seems as if the whole matter is to be forgotten; that all the investigation has been in vain and that the responsibility for what was undoubtedly one of the most ghastly blunders the world has ever know, is never going to be fixed.

WHO IS GUILTY? Can it be possible that the government will take no further step? Those who have been bereaved of dear ones, those who have been disfigured for life, those who now are sightless and those whose homes of happy memories are no more, will have opinions of their own regarding any government which will allow a matter of such tremendous importance to pass without further and drastic action.

No financial aid was available a month later when the preliminary hearing concluded that Mackey was to stand trial for manslaughter, with the added charge of criminal negligence. Again, bail of $6,000 was demanded. This time, since Mackey was unable to pay, he was committed to the common jail on March 6, 1918. One can only imagine the despair he must have experienced at so unexpected an outcome, the distress of his family, the suffering of his children who endured taunts and torment...a nightmare.

At the age of four, Mona would not have felt the full impact of all this public exposure, but she later realized how it affected others in the family. "It must have been a terrible time for Mother," she admitted. "All those headlines blaming my father, all those awful descriptions of people burning to death or with eyes full of glass. And then to have to carry on with five children, another on the way, and her husband in prison and not knowing what would happen to him, or to us! Mother was an incredible woman, what she went through. She must have been so stressed. I think that's what killed her."

In all his visits, Ed was too polite to ask the retired Pilot Mackey directly about his prison experience. But given his preference for careful attire and a well-groomed moustache, Mackey must have found the situation degrading. It is entirely likely he was subjected to abuse from those inmates with nothing left to lose, thanks to the devastation being attributed to his negligence.

Fortunately Mackey's lawyer, Walter O'Hearn, had the wisdom to challenge the legality of the pilot's imprisonment. A writ of *habeas corpus* requires the court to determine immediately whether there is just cause for imprisonment, and if not, to release the prisoner. The case was brought before Judge Benjamin Russell of the Nova Scotia Supreme Court, a thoughtful man unswayed by the clamouring of a public eager to fix blame and demand revenge. O'Hearn argued that a navigator in extreme peril is permitted to do whatever is prudent: "The law did not require Pilot Mackey to wait until he was run into by the other ship, which was not in her proper waters, and he was especially warranted in taking the action he did in view of the cargo he carried."

On March 15, 1918, Judge Russell released Mackey, concluding, "I do not think there is anything at all in the evidence that tends to substantiate the charge of such negligence as would be a necessary ingredient in the crime of manslaughter. I should go further and be inclined to hold that there is not a single fact proved or even stated in the evidence that is not consistent with the exercise of the highest degree of care and thought on the part of the pilot in charge of the *Mont Blanc.*"

It must have distressed Senator Dennis to have the *Halifax Herald* report that outcome on March 16, 1918. Under the headline PILOT MACKEY DISCHARGED, Dennis paid little attention to Judge Russell's defence of Mackey and instead switched focus back to the previous rumours: "Was an Over Patriotic German at the Steamer Imo's Helm, at the Bottom of the Great Catastrophe of December 6th?" Dennis made it appear Mackey was released only because of an affidavit that named Johan Johansen, *Imo's* steersman, as a probable suspect.

Two decades later, after a long and honourable career, Judge Benjamin Russell highlighted this infamous case in his autobiography. Concerning the unjust treatment of Pilot Mackey, Russell writes:

> The event on the harbour gave rise to several indictments and an Inquiry by a commission of which Mr. Justice Drysdale was the President. This Commission took strong grounds against Pilot MacKey [*sic*] placing the responsibility for the collision exclusively upon his shoulders. When Captain MacKey, pilot on board the *Mont Blanc*, was arrested for manslaughter in causing the death of his colleague and others, I was asked to test the matter on the issue of a *habeas corpus*.

It seemed to me that, so far from being negligent or careless, as charged in the information, the defendant had taken every possible care to prevent the collision which was about to be caused by the conduct of the *Imo*....

In fact I went so far in my decision as to say that I even doubted whether any mistake of judgment had been made by the *Mont Blanc*, considering the manner in which she was being crowded over on the Dartmouth shore by the course of the Imo. In any case, it cannot have been manslaughter for a defendant to have done what was best in his judgment to prevent an impending accident, even if, in spite of his best efforts, the struggle was unsuccessful.

Judge Benjamin Russell freed Mackey from prison, declaring there was no evidence of criminal negligence or error on the pilot's part. Nova Scotia Archives

The decision releasing MacKey was probably unpopular. Someone of the infuriated public, meeting one of my boys in the street and unaware of his relation to me, ventured the opinion that I should have been castrated for it.

Francis Mackey was out of prison but not by any means out of the woods. There would be two more failed attempts in the next few weeks to prosecute him, first by Orlando Daniels, Attorney General of Nova Scotia, and then by Andrew Cluny acting on Daniels's behalf. The bitterest blow for Mackey, however, was the discovery that even after his release from jail he was forbidden to have his pilot's license reinstated.

While the preliminary hearing under Magistrate Robert A. Macleod was in progress during February 1918, the federal minister of Marine had launched a separate inquiry into the operation of the pilotage system in Halifax. Strangely enough, there was no reference to the explosion in its five days of hearings and only the *Acadian Recorder* printed brief summaries of each day's testimony. There was, however, plenty of evidence that communication between Halifax and Ottawa had been ragged, and requests for additional pilots and boats had gone unheeded. It was also clear that the pilots were largely ignoring rules and systems proposed by naval authorities. However, during the Wreck Commissioner's Inquiry, the former captain superintendent of the port claimed to have received instructions from Ottawa not to interfere with the pilots.

No final report of the Royal Commission on Pilotage in Halifax was ever published or presented to Parliament, but there exist rare copies of a preliminary report sent to Ottawa a week after the hearings ended; predictably it berated Halifax pilotage for all problems in the harbour. The *Acadian Recorder* was the only local paper covering the hearings and its columns do not give that impression. In fact, its reporting made obvious the major flaws in harbour management and the failure of the federal government to deal with it. Enough evidence had been heard to convince the editors of the *Quebec Telegraph* that "it is upon the authorities that the ultimate onus

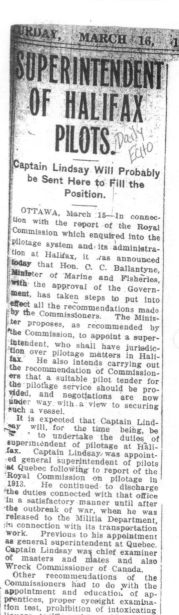

SATURDAY, MARCH 16, 1918

SUPERINTENDENT OF HALIFAX PILOTS. Daily Echo

Captain Lindsay Will Probably be Sent Here to Fill the Position.

OTTAWA, March 15—In connection with the report of the Royal Commission which enquired into the pilotage system and its administration at Halifax, it was announced today that Hon. C. C. Ballantyne, Minister of Marine and Fisheries, with the approval of the Government, has taken steps to put into effect all the recommendations made by the Commissioners. The Minister proposes, as recommended by the Commission, to appoint a superintendent, who shall have jurisdiction over pilotage matters in Halifax. He also intends carrying out the recommendation of Commissioners that a suitable pilot tender for the pilotage service should be provided, and negotiations are now under way with a view to securing such a vessel.

It is expected that Captain Lindsay will, for the time being, be to undertake the duties of superintendent of pilotage at Halifax. Captain Lindsay was appointed general superintendent of pilots at Quebec following to report of the Royal Commission on pilotage in 1913. He continued to discharge the duties connected with that office in a satisfactory manner until after the outbreak of war, when he was released to the Militia Department, in connection with its transportation work. Previous to his appointment as general superintendent at Quebec, Captain Lindsay was chief examiner of masters and mates and also Wreck Commissioner of Canada.

Other recommendations of the Commissioners had to do with the appointment and education of apprentices, proper eyesight examination test, prohibition of intoxicating liquors, tariffs and gratuities.

The Royal Commission has completed its inquiry into conditions at Chatham, Newcastle, Sydney and Louisburg, and will probably open its St. John investigation on Tuesday next.

rests. The captain and pilot were simply instruments of an inexcusably weak and pernicious system...The Minister of Marine is responsible for the negligence of his agents in this matter, and through him the whole Borden government must share the culpability." The Royal Commission's chief recommendation, as expected, was that the minister of Marine take control of pilotage in Halifax. That intent was swiftly confirmed in Ottawa: by Order in Council on March 14, 1918, the Halifax Pilot Commission ceased to exist. Four days later H. St. George Lindsay was appointed superintendent of pilots—and not long afterward would land in hot water because of his sympathy for Mackey's situation.

Sheriff James Hall, chairman of the Halifax Pilot Commission before control was taken over by the federal minister of Marine, C. C. Ballantyne, wrote urgently on March 16, 1918, the day of Mackey's release from prison, asking that Mackey be restored immediately to active service. Five days later came a telegram from Ottawa: "Minister Marine and Fisheries will not approve reinstatement pilot Mackey." No explanation was given. And so began Mackey's long quest to get his license back, and four years of struggling to stay afloat financially.

Lawyer Walter O'Hearn could see how difficult things were for Mackey and his family, and he appealed to Ballantyne to give Mackey a job on the aging Great Lakes steamer *Bayfield*, which was being sent to Halifax to serve as a pilot boat. O'Hearn's letter, written June 6, 1918, included this remarkable plea: "My client feels that his request at the present time to be restored to active duty as a pilot may, perhaps, embarass [*sic*] your department and he fully appreciates the delicacies and niceties of the situation; but he has instructed me to respectfully suggest that in view of the fact that a Pilotage steamer is being provided for this port, he might be given a position on board of her." Apparently the lawyer was aware there would be some resistance to any move that might seem to indicate federal forgiveness of Mackey's supposed sins.

Lindsay, the newly installed superintendent of pilots, believed permission had been granted (the letter of request had been marked "Approved" and initialled by the deputy minister, Alexander Johnston.) Mackey was given command of *Bayfield*. That position lasted only a few weeks, and Lindsay was severely reprimanded, in fact demoted, by officials in Ottawa for hiring the disgraced pilot. It was not a happy experience for Frank Mackey either:

Right in the middle of the fight they put me on an old wreck of a steam pilot boat, that was employed up on the lakes, and appointed me master. I never wanted to go mastering the old thing and just wondered if I should accept that. I knew it was trickery. Well I took charge of her and she lasted about a month, and the last ship I took her out there for I had to coax the engineers to plug the boilers up with rags and try to hold on. There was a sou'easter springing up with snow specks and of course there was a gale after. And the *Olympic* was due off Chebucto Head within an hour. I got word from her.

And now here were the engineers singing out for me to come in, come in, the water was onto the fires. I said, "Is there any possible way you can keep this thing afloat until the *Olympic* gets here? I'd like to get a pilot aboard her. If she comes in here in thick snow it's not going to be good."

Lindsay sped to Ottawa and, having apologized humbly to the federal minister, was restored to his position. *Bayfield* was hauled away for repairs and Captain Mackey was unemployed again.

Mona was still young enough at the time that the full weight of her father's problems didn't overwhelm her. But Ed learned quite a bit about those troubled years during his weekly visits to the retired pilot, and remembered their conversations well.

I heard that plenty of people in the shipping business wrote to the government in Ottawa and asked for that license to be given back but the minister said no. Time and again over the next four years! No reason given. Just told Captain Mackey he should find some other employment. But being a pilot is what he had done all his life and he wasn't trained for anything else.

Not many people these days know that he was stopped from going back to his work after he was released from jail. We in his family never have understood why. He spent all his life's savings in the fight to get his license back. Captain Mackey did his best to keep the family going, with whatever jobs he could pick up taking ships to Saint John or up to Quebec. There was no security, and another new baby, and lawyers to pay.

Mona's little brother Douglas was born in the midst of all those troubles, and do you know, Mrs. Hayes had a son too, Charles, born a few months before the explosion. Those two boys became great friends, went to Tech [Nova Scotia Technical College] at the same time, even went off to Montreal together and lived near each other up there after they were married. I often wonder what conversation Captain Mackey might have had with Mrs. Hayes right after the explosion. But he never spoke of it.

All the while there were still people trying to get him back into court. He never did know why that minister in Ottawa was so dead set on not giving him back his license so he could work as a pilot and earn a proper living. He told me that one time he even went to Ottawa himself to try and see the man in person but never got past his assistant.

Sir Robert Borden, Prime Minister and Member of Parliament for Halifax at the time of the explosion. Nova Scotia Archives

In June 1918 Halifax mayor Arthur Hawkins launched an attempt to appeal Judge Russell's decision to free Mackey. It was denied, but the pressure to punish someone for the explosion remained intense in the city. It is not clear whether that pressure came from federal sources, but it may not be entirely coincidental that Prime Minister Robert Borden had been the Member of Parliament for Halifax until the end of 1917, and that patronage was a way of life in the city, according to observers such as Director of Naval Services Admiral Charles Kingsmill. The admiral perhaps had his own reasons to divert attention from the navy's apparent failure to establish effective controls over harbour movements, a "policeman's job" according to the February 5, 1918, *Ottawa Evening Journal*: "The punishment, the preventive measures for the future must not stop with the prosecution of a pilot, a ship master, and a subordinate examining officer. The horror is too appalling, the measure of official neglect too ghastly."

In October 1918 Halifax's chief of police Frank Hanrahan applied to indict Mackey, with the support of Mayor Hawkins, who had conducted a seven-month campaign to see the pilot's criminal charges reinstated. This renewed attack came just after the birth, on August 9, of Douglas Mackey. In better circumstances it would have

Chief of Police Frank Hanrahan seemed determined to bring Pilot Mackey back before the courts. It is an interesting coincidence that his son grew up close to Pilot Hayes's daughter Agnes and eventually married her in Ottawa, long after Chief Hanrahan's death. NOVA SCOTIA ARCHIVES

been a time for joy. But while this most recent attempt to imprison the pilot also failed, living under such continuous threat was indeed hard on the Mackey family.

"You have to wonder, as the Captain did himself, if there were people in Ottawa too who didn't want to see him set free," Ed mused, "because if he was not to blame, who was responsible? There were already lots of newspaper articles, some of the grandchildren have kept them, and they talk about all the confusion in the harbour and asked who was really supposed to be making the rules and why would such a cargo be allowed to come so close to a city. Easy to blame the pilots if you were looking for a villain and the politicians wanted to hide."

The pilots were, in fact, a prime target for criticism. They were pretty much indifferent to rules imposed by officers of the fledgling Canadian navy whose members they dismissed as inexperienced "prairie chickens," certainly not knowing nearly as much as experienced pilots did about the harbour or the ocean. And, as the inquiry made clear, communication from the Halifax Pilotage Commission office to the navy's Chief Examining Officer aboard *Niobe* had virtually broken down by December of 1917. A fifteen-year-old boy employed by the commission confessed at the inquiry that he had stopped reporting ship movements to that office because he felt his messages were being dismissed and the naval staff were laughing at him. Quite possibly this breakdown contributed to CXO Wyatt's failure to learn that *Imo* had not left Bedford Basin on the afternoon of December 5—at least that was Ed's suspicion.

Meanwhile the owners of *Imo* and *Mont Blanc* had begun suing each other for damages, and the case came before the Nova Scotia Admiralty Division of the Exchequer Court of Canada. As misfortune would have it the judge who presided over that court was Arthur Drysdale. Clearly he should have recused himself from this case, given his obvious bias during the Wreck Commissioner's Inquiry, but he did not. In fact he announced on April 1, 1918, at the beginning of the proceedings, "So far as I am concerned, I have been over it and I have my mind made up, although other witnesses may vary it."

The recorded testimony from the previous inquiry was the only evidence offered, except for the report of one new witness, John L. Makiny, who had testified at the preliminary hearing. Since his opinion was strongly on the side of *Mont Blanc*, Judge Drysdale attacked and discredited him rudely: "Quit talking and listen to the questions!…He is all wrong about the place of collision. It was caused by the improper starboarding of the helm of the *Mont Blanc*. I will file a memorandum!" Drysdale also accused Hector McInnes—now lawyer for *Mont Blanc*, since Humphrey Mellish had meanwhile been appointed a judge—of coaching Makiny to lie. The judge announced his decision on April 27, 1918: he blamed the French vessel entirely and proclaimed that Pilot Mackey's story was absurd.

Mont Blanc's owners immediately appealed the guilty verdict to the Supreme Court of Canada. The same lawyers were on duty: Charles Burchell for *Imo* and Hector McInnes for *Mont Blanc*. The five judges considered all the evidence yet again and came to a different conclusion on May 19, 1919. Two judges blamed *Imo* and two others held *Mont Blanc* to be at fault; the fifth judge believed both ships were in the wrong. The two supporting *Mont Blanc* were crafty enough to realize that the best move was to hold both ships equally responsible. Therefore *Mont Blanc*'s appeal was allowed and neither company was assigned damages or court costs. The next move was *Imo*'s appeal to the Privy Council in Britain, which eventually upheld the decision of the Supreme Court and found both ships to blame for failing to reverse in time to avoid a collision. (Hector McInnes later observed in a letter to the deputy minister that going astern was absolutely not an option for Mackey, as that move would have definitely put *Mont Blanc* in contact with the shore or the harbour bottom, and he had been warned that any such bump could have been disastrous.)

This final decision, issued on March 22, 1920, must have been a blow to Charles Burchell who had gone to London himself, confident he could uphold the total rightness of *Imo*. Now there would be no $2 million award, and no further appeal. The pilot and his lawyers considered Mackey exonerated by the decision and particularly by this statement in the Privy Council's report: "The manoeuvre of the *Mont Blanc* in the agony of the collision may not have been the best manoeuvre to adopt, and yet be in the circumstances excusable." Unfortunately none of these rulings in civil cases provided legal cause for Ballantyne to reverse his administrative decision. There would still be no license for Pilot Mackey.

⚓

Chapter 5

END GAME

June 1919 was a busy month for Mackey's legal team and supporters, now that the Supreme Court had apparently cleared the pilot of blame for the collision. Immediately the letters and appeals to Minister of Marine Ballantyne multiplied and their language became much stronger. Halifax senator William Roche pointed out to the minister on July 3, 1919, that Pilot Mackey had been severely punished already, and unfairly. Even Alexander Johnston, the deputy minister of Marine, wrote a note to Ballantyne recommending approval for the reinstatement of Mackey's license. The pilots were in favour of Mackey's return to service, and the federal superintendent of pilotage, G. E. L. Robertson, told the minister there was unanimous support for Mackey on account of his long years of satisfactory service. Encouraged, the stranded pilot sent a plea for a meeting with Robertson.

> Halifax Sept. 30th, 1919
> Capt. G. E. L. Robertson,
> Gen. Supt. of Pilots, Ottawa
>
> Dear Sir,
> As I have been informed that you are coming to Halifax soon, on business in connection with pilotage matters, I desire to place before you some facts concerning my case. I presume it has been brought to your

attention ere this, but not hearing from the Marine Dept., I decided to write you.

I was pilot of the French steamer *Mont Blanc*, which blew up in Halifax Harbour, after being in collision with the Norwegian steamer Imo, on the sixth of December 1917; an inquiry was held shortly after, and the *Mt. Blanc* held to blame, the Captain and myself were arrested on a charge of manslaughter. I immediately engaged counsel, and my case was tried by one of our most learned Judges, Judge Russell, who discharged me on a writ of *habeas corpus*, as there was no evidence to warrant an indictment, or trial by jury.

Later on, some prejudiced individuals tried to get the Attorney General to indict me but he refused, saying that Judge Russell's decision was quite sufficient; they tried other schemes to have me tried by jury, but failed miserably.

I was vindicated four times in the courts, and once by a bench of judges. My vindication automatically cleared the French Captain and he went home to France, where soon after arriving he was exonerated by the Admiralty and his company, the Generale Transatlantique steamship company, and placed in command of another ship, the s s *Garrone*.

Later the French company appealed their case to the Supreme Court of Canada, and the Halifax decisions given at the inquiry and Admiralty courts were reversed, both ships were held liable for damages. The Chief Justice of Canada exonerated me, saying that the captain gave the order on his own responsibility and not on the advice of his pilot.

I have had my solicitor write the Minister of Marine, Mr. Ballantyne, and sent him a petition signed by the leading steamship agents of Halifax, strongly recommending my reinstatement in the pilot service. Captain Henry, supt. of pilots here, has also written recommending it. All I have heard so far is that the letters have been acknowledged.

I have a wife and six young children to support, and find it very hard indeed as I have no permanent employment and have been subject to heavy legal expenses. I have spent the best of my life in the pilot service and consequently have not fitted myself for any other occupation, not having any opportunity to do so.

I venture to state that if you should happen to inquire you will find that I have always tried to give good satisfaction as a pilot, wherever employed. I have been employed as special pilot by different companies and there were never any complaints.

Having been under suspension since January 1918 and having undergone considerable persecution during that time, and at last exonerated, I hereby ask you to give this your kindest consideration, and favour me by doing all you can towards reinstating me in the pilot service again.

Hoping to hear from you, or see you in Halifax, I remain

Yours faithfully,
Francis Mackey

Robertson's rueful reply was that despite his best efforts on the pilot's behalf, he could hold out no hope for reinstatement. And so it went with every other attempt Mackey made to see justice done during the next two years.

Mona was quick to point out that her father could have left Halifax:

> There were relatives out west, but he wanted to stay right here and not look shamefaced by running away. My father took whatever work he could find, not as a pilot but taking boats along the coast. It wasn't

Mona's grandfather Captain Michael Wrayton.

anywhere close to what a pilot would earn. I didn't think we were poor. Maybe we were! It seemed like we always had enough to eat, but I think my mother's family might have helped us out a bit. They lived on Queen Street. Her father was a sea captain on the *Ocean Belle*: Captain Wrayton, a great supporter of the Irish cause, and I remember he used to bring us special biscuits made by his ship's cook. But the Wraytons weren't in favour of Father spending all that money on lawyers.

Halifax, N.S.,
April 19, 1920.

The Hon. The Minister of Marine,
    Ottawa, Ont.

Dear Sir:

    The undersigned persons, interested in the shipping business of the port of Halifax, respectfully petition you to consider the application of former pilot Frank Mackey for reinstatement.

    The most helpful reason that we can advance for your favourable action in respect to this matter, is the decision of the Privy Council, which has affirmed that of the Supreme Court of Canada, in which Sir Louis Davies, Chief Justice, exonerates pilot Mackey from all blame.

    We feel that the litigation in connection with this unfortunate occurrence of December 6th, 1917, having been finally ended, that the facts have been fully ascertained, and we feel that it is only justice to Mr. Mackey to replace him in his former position.

The original copy has been signed by all the shipping people of Halifax

Francis Mackey was indeed spending much of his life's savings on lawyers in the vain attempt to return to his proper profession; their efforts produced a flood of letters and petitions, all to no avail. Support came from all the major shipping agents with traffic in the Halifax Harbour, clearly expressing their need for the services of this highly skilled pilot whose competence had been proven to them over many years of association. They also expressed the view, in a preamble to one of their urgent petitions, that furious public sentiment had calmed down in Halifax and that there would be no opposition to Mackey's reinstatement.

Still, not much changed in the desperate situation of the Mackey family. His long absences from home, as a master "taking ships around the coast, sometimes to Boston, Portland, Montreal, Quebec, Sydney, Louisburg, Saint John, and other places," did not come close to providing the income he would have earned in his proper role as a harbour pilot.

The only opportunity the pilot had to state his case directly came in December of 1920, when Ballantyne visited Halifax and allowed Mackey a brief interview. Apparently the minister indicated he would respond promptly to the pilot's plea but did not keep that promise. As Mackey explained much later to some of his faithful supporters, Ballantyne "did not bother his hand, so I went away to Newfoundland, in an American tug to tow a ship from St. John's to Norfolk. I was away about a month and when I came back there was no letter from him, so I wrote him immediately and got an evasive reply."

> Halifax Mar 2, 1921
> Hon. C. C. Ballantyne
> Minister of Marine
>
> Dear Sir
>
> Since meeting you at the Halifax Hotel when you were here in December last, and after discussing matters pertaining to my reinstatement in the pilot service, I have been anxiously waiting to hear from you as you said when you went back to Ottawa you would consider everything and write me the following week.
>
> So I have been wondering whether a letter from you had been mislaid or gone astray, or if you have had time to go into the matter. I know

that you must be kept busy from time to time, a fact which would cause some delay concerning my affairs. But I would sincerely appreciate any encouraging news from you, favouring my reinstatement.

I have a wife, and family of six children, to support, and I am out of employment; and the outlook is very dark and looking worse from day to day. I do not care to go into details concerning this. I presume you can imagine what it is like. Trusting you will give this your favourable consideration.

I am
Yours respectfully

Francis Mackey

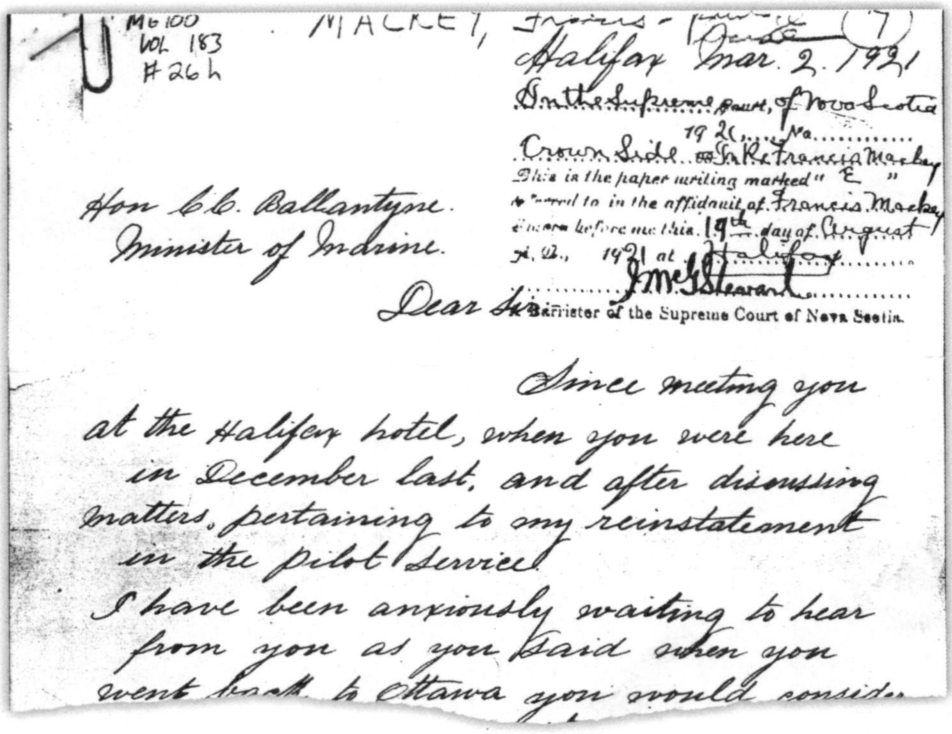

This time Ballantyne actually concluded he ought to respond. Two weeks later he sent a letter announcing he had examined the case thoroughly from every possible angle, and "While I am not unmindful of the hardship which followed the cancellation of your Pilot's Certificate, I regret to say that I have been unable to reach a conclusion that would warrant my deciding to restore your license."

Unwittingly Ballantyne had in fact helped Mackey with this reply, as it provided evidence the minister considered the license *cancelled*. Indeed that was certainly what the bloody-minded Wreck Commissioner Louis Demers had strongly advised in his letter to Alex Johnston, March 21, 1918:

> I may state that Judge Drysdale had the power to cancel Mackay's [*sic*] license, which should have been done. Now that the Commission of Pilotage is abolished, it seems to me that the Minister can rectify the error made by Judge Drysdale and cancel Mackay's license, on the ground of gross error of judgment. His liberation on the manslaughter charge does not affect the situation as to his default as a Pilot, in violating the Rules of the Road.

Under the terms of the Canada Shipping Act it was decreed that no master's, mate's, pilot's, or engineer's license could be cancelled before he had been given an opportunity to defend himself in a proper investigation. No such opportunity had been provided to Mackey: he had not even been officially summoned to the

Charles C. Ballantyne, minister of Marine and Fisheries and of Naval Services in the Borden cabinet.

Drysdale Inquiry but had gone there voluntarily to provide information. The fact that Ballantyne used the word "cancellation" in his only written reply to the appeals gave lawyer L. A. Forsyth excellent ammunition. "Now my license was never cancelled, but he thought it was. However he showed his ignorance to the Canada Shipping Act," Mackey explained in a letter to his supporters at the Navigator's Federation.

With this written evidence from Ballantyne in hand, in the summer of 1921 the Halifax lawyer decided to threaten the minister with serious legal action since all amicable means to secure the return of the certificate had failed. In August Mackey signed a sworn deposition reviewing the history of the case and pointing out the ways his rights had been violated:

> I attended as a witness at the Inquiry and gave evidence but no charge was formulated against me, nor was I furnished with a copy of the report or a statement of the case on which this investigation was ordered. Nor was I given an opportunity to make a defence since no charge against me had been called to my attention. On the enquiry I was not represented by counsel. I believe that the cancellation of my certificate is illegal and unwarranted on the grounds that the provisions of the Merchant's Shipping Act were not complied with.

Forsyth actually got to the point of serving notice to the minister of Marine that the Nova Scotia Supreme Court would be asked to challenge the decision of Judge Drysdale. However, before the legal challenge could get under way, there came about finally a resolution that did not involve the courts but the ballot box.

The federal election of December 1921 brought about a change of government, and C. C. Ballantyne suffered a stunning defeat in his own riding. The newly crowned Liberal prime minister, William Lyon MacKenzie King, appointed his trusted Quebec stalwart, Ernest Lapointe, as minister of Marine and Fisheries. As one of his first acts in office, Lapointe with no hesitation restored the long-denied pilot's license.

The official letter with the crest of Canada at the top above "Department Of Marine" became a family treasure, which I now have the honour to preserve.

Dated February 10, 1922, it came from Superintendent of Pilots H. St. George Lindsay, who had certainly been among those supporters urging the minister to relent during the previous four years. It must have brought him considerable satisfaction to write,

Pilotage File No. ....

Marine Dept. File No. ....

CANADA

DEPARTMENT OF MARINE

SUPERINTENDENT OF PILOTS

AT Halifax, N. S., Feb. 10, 19 22.

Mr. Frank Mackey,
    382 Robie St.,
        City.

Dear Sir:-

I am advised from Ottawa, that you will be restored to your former position, in good standing, as a pilot, in the Halifax Pilotage District, provided you first pass successfully the necessary tests for eyesight and hearing.-

If you will arrange to call at this office on Monday, 13th, (providing it is a bright day) and pass the examination above mentioned, I shall have the pleasure of handing you your license, which has been forwarded from the Department, this day.-

Yours truly,

H St G Lindsay
Supt.

(Capt. H.St.G. Lindsay)
Supt. of Pilots.

*Recd License
on Feb 14th
Valentines day
1922*

I am advised from Ottawa that you will be restored to your former position, in good standing, as a pilot, in the Halifax Pilotage District, provided you first pass successfully the necessary tests for eyesight and hearing.

If you will arrange to call at this office on Monday, 13th, (providing it is a bright day) and pass the examination above mentioned, I shall have the pleasure of handing you your license, which has been forwarded from the Department, this day.

Inscribed on the bottom of the letter in Mackey's own bold hand is the note: "Recd License on Feb 14th Valentines day 1922."

As Mona handed the letter to me for safekeeping she commented there was more to that part of the story, because when the shiny new piece of paper arrived her father scorned it. "Father said, 'This is not the license I've been fighting for.' Turns out that when he was first sent to court he took his license to the pilot office and hid it between a couple of books on a shelf. He cut a little piece off the edge of it so he would know it was his. He got the original one back! Finally

PILOT MACKEY REINSTATED

His License Returned and He Will Now Resume Duty.

Francis Mackey, who was pilot on the death ship Mont Blanc, in Halifax harbor on Dec. 6th, 1917, and whose license was withheld from him following investigation into the collision between that steamer and the steamer Imo which resulted in the fatal explosion on that morning, has been reinstated, it became known yesterday. The pilot, after fighting his case for four years in the courts, is naturally gratified at the outcome and his friends yesterday were congratulating him on his success.

The order for the pilots' reinstatement came to Superintendent of Pilots Lindsay, from the Minister of Marine at Ottawa, requiring the restoration of the pilot to his former position as such and in good standing. Yesterday Pilot

Mackey took the eye test and was found perfect—100 per cent.

The story of the pilot's fight for reinstatement is a lengthy one, but a summary of it is interesting. When he was arrested on Feb. 6th, 1918, on a charge of manslaughter, a similiar charge being preferred against the Captain of the Mont Blanc, Pilot Mackey handed in his license to the Halifax Pilotage Commission, then supervising the pilots here, on the understanding, he says, that it would be returned if he were acquitted. When Judge Russell dismissed the case on habeas corpus proceedings, it was not returned, the license being held, the pilot understood, on orders from Hon. C. C. Ballantyne, then Minister of Marine.

Prior to that, the Wreck Commissioners Court, at Halifax, especially appointed soon after the explosion to investigate the collision which caused the disaster, in the course of its finding blaming the Mont Blanc for the collision, recommended cancellation of Pilot Mackey's license. From the Admiralty Court here the case went to the Supreme Court of Canada, two

judges of which blamed the Mont Blanc, two blamed the Imo, and a fifth found both equally responsible, Chief Justice Sir Louis Davies, in the cause of his decision, giving the opinion that Pilot Mackey was not to blame. The case then went to the Privy Council, which found both ships at fault.

Late last year, L. A. Forsythe, acting for the pilot, applied for a writ of certiorari to bring the finding of the Wreck Commissioners' Court, recommending cancellation of the pilot's license, before the Supreme Court here on the grounds that the proceedings of the Wreck Commissioners were invalid. Judge Russell, before whom the application was made, granted an order nisi for a writ calling on the Department of Marine to show cause why the proceedings should not be quashed.

Before the matter was scheduled to come up for final argument, the Department of Marine decided to reinstate the pilot, and he now resumes his duties. His license was never cancelled and has been returned to him after four years shelving in the local pilot office.

The Morning Chronicle, *February 15, 1922.*

there was a good headline in the paper: PILOT MACKEY REINSTATED!"

Mona had a copy of another treasured letter, sent to her mother, Lillian, when the good news reached the west coast. "We heard from his mother, Sarah, that they had a great party of celebration out there and put his picture on the mantel so he could see all the commotion. Dancing and card playing and food and music until one in the morning. She sent a prayer that 'there should be no more wars or war accidents so long as this old world lasts.'" Mona, like the pilot's mother, believed none of this trouble would have happened if there had been no war.

Finally, instead of composing humble pleas to the politicians who had held such power over his life, Francis Mackey was free to speak his mind about the ordeal, and he did so promptly in a letter of thanks to one of the many groups who had supported him through the "long, long fight."

Sarah Mackey, the pilot's mother, celebrated the restoration of the pilot's license with family in British Columbia.

Canadian Navigators Federation
March 1922

I am sure you have a good idea of the heavy load that was placed upon my shoulders by that unjust court of inquiry, and as you know they were a bunch of piratical manipulators and their sole purpose was to save the blundering Canadian Navy and make a victim of somebody else.

However, when they had me arrested for manslaughter I immediately began the long, long fight, first in the lower courts and then in the highest courts of the land, in order to eliminate that malicious miscarriage of justice and vindicate myself in the good old fashioned style.

During that four long years, mostly all persecution and meeting many pessimists, even among my relatives, made my load seem very heavy indeed, but I seemed to get more determination and backbone than I thought I could ever possess, and I used to always say to them "I see the word VICTORY before me and nothing else."

Now after four years, the mills of justice grinding exceedingly slow, but sure, it is now very gratifying to me to tell you, dear brothers, that I have beaten them all to the dust, and come through it all victorious, and with perfect eyesight and my license returned.

Yet there was still a great injustice Mackey sought to correct. He requested compensation for the years of wrongfully lost wages, hoping to recover $17,000, which would have been his income as a pilot, instead of the $1,700 he'd managed to earn with occasional work. His appeal was denied. Ironically Ballantyne, who had prevented Mackey from returning to the pilotage, was eventually rewarded with a senator's pay. He was already a wealthy businessman, and in fact had spent $40,000 on his unsuccessful re-election campaign. Mackey, on the other hand, had struggled to meet his family's needs and the legal expenses incurred during those four long years.

Typical of Mackey's honest character, it was most important to him that every penny of those lawyers' fees be paid back, though it would take him six years. Mona remembers walking every week to Davison and Forsyth's office with an envelope of money; the final one, saved in family files, was dated in Mackey's hand, "April 1928 Last Payment $12.69."

Chapter 6

⚓

THE AFTERMATH

Mackey's sense of vindication and restored pride must have been almost as important to him as the easing of his financial worries. Clearly his good reputation was vital to him and it had been badly battered. As long as he was forbidden to resume his work as a pilot he continued to be a tarnished suspect, though he steadfastly refused to accept shame as his due. There was very likely an east coast victory party too, of at least as much merriment as his mother reported from Vancouver, and with the pilot himself in the midst of it rather than watching from the mantel.

But the celebration didn't last long. As Mona explained, by this time her mother, Lillian, Mackey's beloved wife, was failing: "I knew something was wrong but nobody ever told me how bad it was. After a while she was in bed most of the time but we could still talk and tell stories and so on." Then one day in January of 1924, nine-year-old Mona came home from school to find some black crepe on the door, and her mother's sisters in the kitchen with big pots of dye on the stove, turning everybody's clothes black. "I imagine all the troubles had been too hard on my mother," added Mona. "She had six children and she had to go through all that explosion thing, and even when my father was cleared he still couldn't work. She was only forty-seven when she died and I think all that stress had some bearing on it."

Still with sadness in her voice, Mona continued,

> My father took me down to Wood Brothers to buy a nice dress, and to the shoe store, but that time doesn't seem real, or I just couldn't take it in. Douglas was still pretty young, just five.
>
> Father couldn't afford to take much time off. The pilots had to go out on the pilot boat for a week at a time so Father was going to need help at home and I think he was keen to get rid of my mother's sisters who were there at first. Doug told one of his children a story about that. Once when Father came home from the pilot boat Douglas was too sore to sit down, and Father found out one of the aunts had spanked him with a hairbrush, and that did it. Gone.
>
> For a while we had a housekeeper from down Sambro way but my father must have put an ad in the paper for a new one. I remember sitting at the top of the stairs with Doug when he was interviewing. You know how kids are, they want to listen and see what's going on. There was one lady came in first and then a second one but we voted for the first. He made us feel our opinion was really important.
>
> My father called the first lady, who had something to do with the children's hospital, and he wanted her but he couldn't get hold of her. So he called the next one and she moved in. She had a grown-up son, about seventeen or eighteen, Gerard Dobson. He came to live with us too and my father got him a job on one of the cable ships, but he got really seasick and then he went to work on the trams.

Margaret Mary Dunne Dobson had migrated with her family from Newfoundland to the Boston area, and her early days are somewhat of a mystery. Photographs of her elegant self and well-dressed son, Gerard, were taken in New York in 1914, but she apparently lived in Charlotte, North Carolina, for the next three years. She crossed into Nova Scotia on the Yarmouth ferry after her divorce from Reginald Dobson in 1917, leaving her then ten-year-old son in a Massachusetts orphanage until she could afford to send for him. At the time of answering the ad for a housekeeper in the Mackey home, she was working for an apple farmer in the Annapolis Valley.

Margaret was a tall and attractive woman, obviously strengthened by her own challenging life experiences. The prospect of taking on a household with young children for a widower who would be away on a pilot boat every second week would have been daunting otherwise. There is no record of the interview or what further conversations took place between the pilot and the newcomer. She certainly would have been aware of his troubles over the past six years, but whether she would have shared her own is an intriguing question.

Photos of Margaret Dobson and her son, Gerard, taken in New York, 1914.

In September of 1925 the two were married. By this time some of the Mackey children were old enough to be on their own. Ed observed it must have been hard for them to lose their real mother and then have a different one so soon. But he supposed at that time the Captain felt getting married would have been the proper thing to do, and he believed the couple had a loving relationship. "When I used to visit them later it seemed they got along, bantering a bit when he annoyed her."

Mona's recollections of her new stepmother were less positive. "She had her good points, but she was so different from my mother. I didn't mind it so much as my sister Marjorie and the older ones did. Marjorie was nearly ten when the explosion happened. The older ones took more in and they were hurt by all of it, people talking, so they never wanted to hear anything more about it. Too hurtful. They left home, mostly, but Douglas and I had no choice." Mona did however agree with Ed that there had to be a prompt solution to the pilot's domestic dilemma. "I guess Father had realized the youngest ones still needed mothering so that's likely why he married her. He was a good father, very strict, but he made time for us on the

Cpt Frank Mackey   Margaret Mackey (Dunn)

Captain Mackey with his second wife, Margaret Dunn Dobson Mackey.

weeks he was home. He'd always take us to the circus, and he took me to Mahone Bay when they were building a new pilot schooner, to see how it was coming. That was the *Hebridean* and he was voted captain of it by the other pilots."

Clearly Mona held a special place in Francis Mackey's world, though he also had a close relationship with his oldest son, Ronald. Mona remembered with pleasure the times her father was at home and able to be part of their growing up.

When I got a bit older I loved to be on stage. There were quite a few groups like the Children of Mary, and the Knights of Columbus sponsored some. Then I got into the drama guild at the church started by Dr. Burns. He was a priest at St. Mary's. One play I remember best was called *You Can't Beat the Irish!* and I still know all the lines. I came to life out of a picture. Father came to see one of my plays and I could see him down in the audience laughing, and afterward he gave me a hug. He was not what you would call demonstrative in public. Quite reserved and dignified. But he did give us children hugs.

Denied compensation for lost wages, Francis Mackey had no choice but to keep working until he reached the age of sixty-five, in 1937. It is unlikely, however, that he would have given up sooner even if financial need had not been a factor. Mackey was a proud man. He served as captain of *Hebridean* on the weeks it was his turn to wait off Chebucto Head with a group of seven or eight pilots who would rotate the duties as ships entered or left the harbour.

On Captain Mackey's sixty-fifth birthday, November 1, 1937, notice came that his license was now expired,

Mackey on the deck of *Hebridean*, launched in 1928.

83

Mackey's license restored in 1922, signed by the new minister of Marine, Ernest Lapointe, cancelled in 1937 and replaced by a temporary license.

but he could apply for a temporary license if he passed, again, the competency tests. Defiantly he took those tests and passed easily, but, having proven his point, he announced at the end of November that he really didn't want to deal with the icy challenge of another winter on the ocean. His fellow pilots had, a decade earlier, granted him full pension coverage for the four lost years and they were still paying a small pension, $264 yearly, to the widow of William Hayes. Francis Mackey applied for superannuation after forty-two years of dedicated service.

Superintendent-General of Pilotage G. E. L. Robertson accepted the retirement request and confirmed Mackey was entitled to a full pension of $1,600 per annum. His fellow pilots agreed he should receive three months' retirement leave plus a share of any surplus until February 28, 1938. Robertson wrote, "Please convey to Mr. Mackey the appreciation of the Department, and my personal appreciation, of his long years of service in the Halifax Pilotage Service."

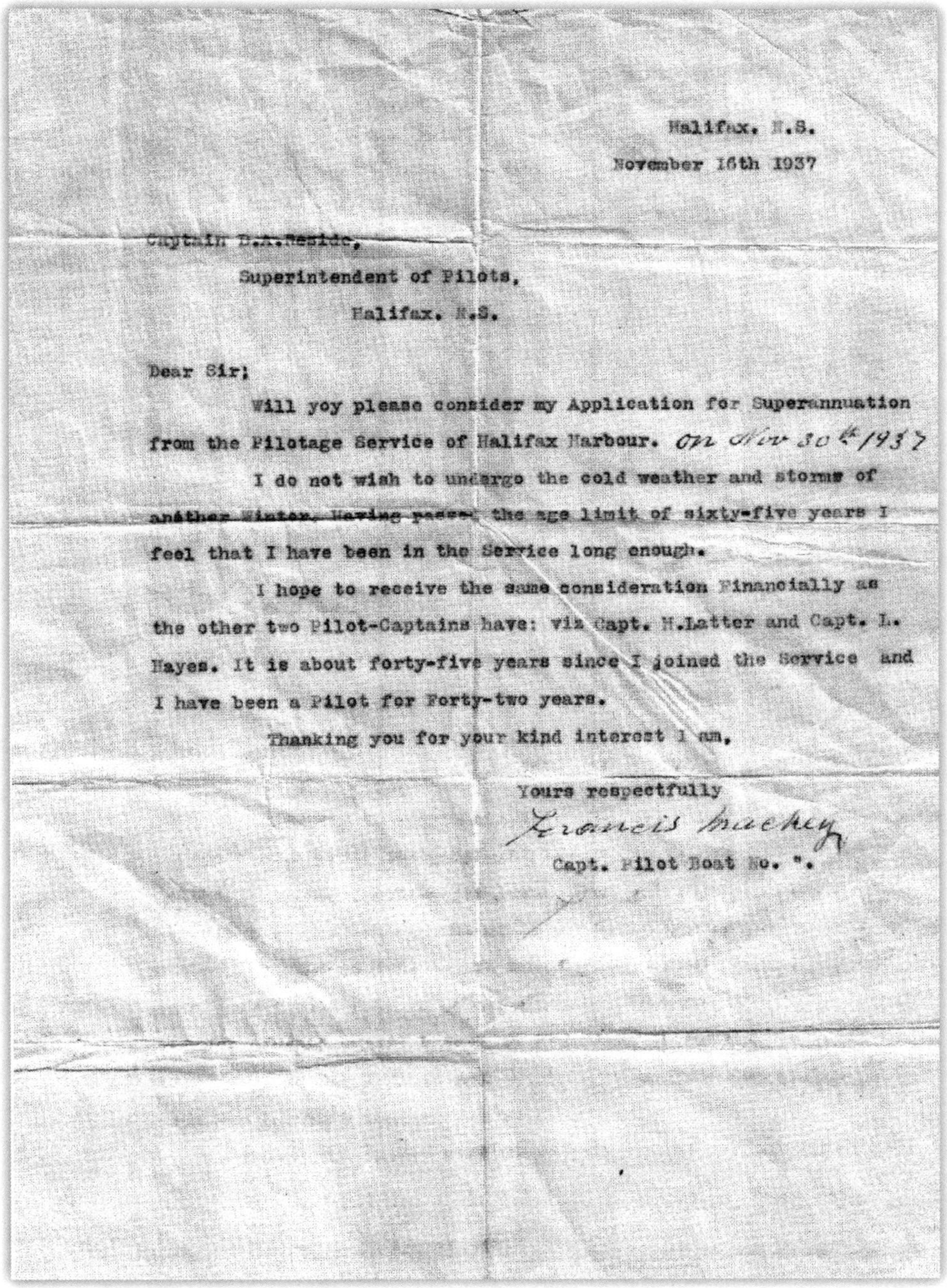

Halifax, N.S.

November 16th 1937

Captain D.A.Reside,

Superintendent of Pilots,

Halifax, N.S.

Dear Sir;

Will yoy please consider my Application for Superannuation
from the Pilotage Service of Halifax Harbour. *On Nov 30th 1937*

I do not wish to undergo the cold weather and storms of
another Winter. Having passed the age limit of sixty-five years I
feel that I have been in the Service long enough.

I hope to receive the same consideration Financially as
the other two Pilot-Captains have: viz Capt. H.Latter and Capt. L.
Hayes. It is about forty-five years since I joined the Service and
I have been a Pilot for Forty-two years.

Thanking you for your kind interest I am,

Yours respectfully

Francis Mackey

Capt. Pilot Boat No. ".

It turned out Mackey could adapt to retirement quite happily, and managed to fill another twenty-four years with new accomplishments. If he had any regrets at the end of his challenging career they were not evident. In fact when he was offered a chance to pilot the ship bringing King George and Queen Elizabeth into Halifax in 1939 he refused the honour, saying it ought to be given to a currently serving pilot.

Then in March of 1940 came a night when regret might well have dominated Mackey's thinking, as the pilot schooner *Hebridean* met a terrible fate. Rammed by an incoming British freighter, *Hebridean* sank within minutes, drowning six of Mackey's fellow pilots and three crew members. Their bodies and the schooner itself were never found, and in that instant thirty-five Herring Cove children were left fatherless. If Captain Mackey had been in charge that night, would he have been able to avoid the collision? The inquiry into this tragedy was not made public at the time, since it occurred near the beginning of the Second World War and security demanded secrecy. Indeed the investigation would draw no definite conclusion, since the only survivors had been in a rowboat at the time of the collision, delivering a pilot to the freighter, or asleep below decks and tossed

Hebridean leaving Herring Cove (MacAskill's *Rainbow at Night*). NOVA SCOTIA ARCHIVES

into the shock of cold black water. It was suggested that perhaps the *Hebridean*'s diesel engine failed just as was crossing in front of the incoming vessel, a standard maneuver to pick up the small boat and crew. Nobody suggested pilot error.

According to his daughter, when he was not on the water Mackey preferred the country to city life, and always had a cabin or shack out by the shore. He owned quite a bit of land out Harrietsfield way, Mona recalled, and shared a cabin with his eldest son, Ronnie, in Tantallon where he could go fishing. Once he retired he started building a house in Spryfield, which was country back then. Some of the Dobson grandchildren describe the house as quite elegant, in particular the green marble bathroom, and former neighbour Gordon Macintyre admired the expanse of beautiful lawns and gardens surrounding it:

> In 1946, as a boy of five years of age, I moved with my family from the north end of Halifax to LeMarchant Street in Spryfield. Our home was across the street from the Mackey home, a lovely, stately two-storey with a large garage. The property was bounded on all sides by an ornate white fence, with gates both to the garage and to the home. The latter was adorned with a trellised arch, and opened onto a cement walkway. The property was always well groomed, grass well cut and maintained, with very pretty flower beds here and there to further adorn the property. There was also an attractive stone well on the left front of the property, just inside the fence. All the work on the property was done by Captain Mackey. He was a hardworking man, regularly seen out in the yard cutting, pruning, and keeping the place "ship shape," so to speak.

Treasuring his memories, MacIntyre spoke fondly of a warm connection between the two families: "Mrs. Mackey was a lovely person, and she and my mom developed a friendly relationship; they were often chatting and being neighbourly. The depth of this friendship was shown when Mrs. Mackey agreed to be the baptismal godmother for my younger sister, Margaret, nicknamed 'Margo,' who was named after Mrs. Mackey."

Once the home was complete, Mackey proceeded to create with his own hands that wishing well on the lawn. He left the Robie Street house to Ronnie

In Spryfield Mackey
was a keen gardener,
"keeping the place
ship-shape."

Captain Mackey and Margaret enjoyed travels from east coast to the far west: Mackey, Mona, Rita Simmons, Nana (Margaret), and Douglas on an adventure, perhaps 1927/28. Margaret is protective of Douglas who had really known only her as mother.

A visit with the pilot's mother in British Columbia: Mackey, his sister Mary Ellen, Sarah Mackey, and a massive Douglas Fir.

Mackey and Margaret at Sheet Harbour falls.

The Spryfield house and much admired handmade wishing well.

and in the mortgage negotiations for the new Spryfield dwelling had Ronnie sign for him. Francis Mackey always paid cash for everything, even in the darkest time, and had no credit history.

"I think he surprised himself liking retirement so much," Mona admitted. "Father learned to paint, carved ships, went fishing, told stories to anyone who would listen, and read plenty of books." One of the treasured volumes in his collection was an autographed copy of Eleanor Roosevelt's 1949 memoirs, "Inscribed for Captain Frank Mackey with best wishes."

The veteran storyteller also spoke at length to author Michael Bird, who would go on to write *The Town that Died*. "That book didn't come out until quite a few years after Father was gone so I don't know what he would have thought of it," said Mona. "I think Mr. Bird took liberties with my father's words. Father certainly was not one to swear like that and he was never afraid of anything." Mona sadly recalled that other publications, even *Reader's Digest*, copied from Bird's 1962 book as if it were gospel. She produced an envelope of clippings from a British newspaper, the *Sunday Express* of March 1962, which had

Arthur Lismer's famed painting of legendary ocean liner turned troop ship RMS *Olympic*, still in dazzle, returning war-weary soldiers to Halifax in 1919; the devastated city's docks were now back in operation, a welcome sight at last.

Arthur Lismer
Olympic with Returned Soldiers
CWM 19710261-0343
Beaverbrook Collection of War Art
Canadian War Museum.

The wishing well and retirement home Francis Mackey built in Spryfield 1938–39, surrounded with well-kept gardens.

In Beauharnois, Quebec, the retirement home of the pilot's sister Loretta, famously known as Aunt Babe, but a mystery to the Mackeys next door: Denyse, Frank, and Laurette, who welcomed me and shared many family documents (2007).

AMY JENSEN

TOP Pilot Mackey's pocketwatch and Bible in the hands of his grandson Frank Mackey.

LEFT Pilot Hayes's watch, damaged by the explosion, was given to his son Charles and is now kept safe by his granddaughter in Ottawa.

BOTTOM LEFT In Herring Cove stands this striking monument to Pilot William Hayes, joined fifty years later by his widow, Gertrude.

BOTTOM RIGHT Francis Mackey's gravestone in Mount Olivet cemetery, Halifax, includes the record of two wives and a daughter.

TOP Shard of *Mont Blanc* found in the garden of the Cabot Street house by Percy Simmons, now in a memorial park opposite Blessed Mother Theresa Church.

BOTTOM This monument to the firemen killed attempting to douse the flames on Mont Blanc stands in front of Fire Station #4, Duffus Street at Robie. BARBARA DeLORY

TOP *Mont Blanc*'s huge anchor shaft flew four kilometres across the city and the Northwest Arm, landing on the Edmonds grounds. BOTTOM In the Hydrostone Park, this marker shows the direction and distance to ground zero, and plaques celebrate the rebuilding of Richmond.

A pilot's challenges: inside the harbour (the Narrows, where the 1917 Halifax Explosion happened) and outside, where even on a fine day the ocean can be rough. APA Deckhand Jason Coakley captured the drama of transferring a pilot at the harbour entrance. Atlantic Pilotage Authority, 2011

Ted Dykstra imaginatively portrays Pilot Mackey in the miniseries *Shattered City*, 2003. "That's not Grandpa!" DAN CALLIS.

A real pilot, Captain Ian Swan, quietly at work on the bridge of an incoming foreign vessel. ATLANTIC PILOTAGE AUTHORITY

The Atlantic Pilotage Authority created a memorial in Herring Cove to the nine pilots and crew lost when the pilot schooner *Hebridean* was struck by a British freighter, March 28, 1940. Francis Mackey had supervised the construction of this much-needed pilot boat, launched in 1928 and under his command much of the time until his retirement in November of 1937. The village of Herring Cove produced whole families of pilots, and they often sailed from this protected harbour out to meet incoming ships at the pilot station off Chebucto Head, the point of land visible on the horizon. Mackey boarded the ill-fated *Mont Blanc* there on the afternoon of December 5, 1917.